THE
INTERNATIONAL
SCHOOL OF

SUGARCRAFT

BOOK ONE
BEGINNERS

THE
INTERNATIONAL
SCHOOL OF
SUGARCRAFT

BOOK ONE
BEGINNERS

Principal Teacher: Nicholas Lodge
Teacher: Janice Murfitt
Photography by Graham Tann

MEREHURST

LONDON

Published 1988 by Merehurst Limited
Ferry House, 51/57 Lacy Road,
London SW15 1PR

© Copyright 1988 Merehurst Limited

Reprinted 1989, 1990 (twice), 1991, 1992 (twice), 1993, 1996
ISBN 1 85391 493 2

A catalogue record for this book is available from the British Library.

Edited by Deborah Gray
Designed by Richard Slater
Photography by Graham Tann, assisted by Lucy Baker and Hilary Slater
Typeset by Angel Graphics
Colour separation by Fotographics Ltd, U.K. – Hong Kong
Printed in Italy by New Interlitho S.p.A., Milan

ACKNOWLEDGEMENTS
I would like to dedicate this book to Sindy for being a loving and understanding
wife. My thanks to Janice Murfitt for the first section of this beautiful book; to
Martin Northcote for cutting the boards shown in lesson three; to Lucy Baker
and Hilary Slater for all their help and preparation in the studio; to Graham
Tann for all his patience; to Monica and David for all their help in the
preparation of the cakes featured; to Brenda Tyler for typing up all my notes; to
B.R. Mathews and J.F. Renshaw & Company Limited for all the equipment and
help given.

The Publishers would like to thank the following for their help and advice:

Clay gun kindly supplied by Briar Wheels & Supplies Limited, Whitsbury Road,
Fordingbridge, Hants. SP6 1NQ
Mavis Giles
Suzan and Pepe Lara Matheu
B.R. Mathews & Son, 12 Gipsy Hill, Upper Norwood, London SE19 1NN
Ribbons from C.M. Offray & Son Limited, Firtree Place, Church Road,
Ashford, Middlesex CW15 2PH
Those products supplied by John F. Renshaw & Company Limited are readily
available from your local sugarcraft shop in the U.K., or by contacting John F.
Renshaw & Company Limited, Locks Lane, Mitcham, Surrey for overseas orders
Tate & Lyle, Enterprise House, 45 Homesdale Road, Bromley BR2 9TE

INTRODUCTION

This is the first of two books in The International School of Sugarcraft. The aim of the series is twofold: firstly, to provide a clear and concise course for the beginner; and secondly, to supply the more experienced cake decorator with a comprehensive and instructive reference work.

The book begins with the basics, with information and delicious recipes for cakes and an excellent selection of icings, marzipans and sugarpastes for all occasions. The course then introduces the skills of piping, runout and extension work, lettering, sugar moulding and modelling, to mention but a few. Each chapter is fully illustrated with colour photographs, step-by-step instructions and templates, where necessary and builds up to a feature cake that may be decorated once the skills in the chapter are mastered. The chapters towards the end of the book do suppose an understanding of the skills introduced in the earlier lessons.

Cake decorating, like any craft, relies on design, that nebulous combination of colour, texture and shape that may be taught, but can only be mastered by experience. This book features chapters on design which discuss the specific considerations that must be taken into account when planning a cake. However, the entire book may be seen as a lesson in design as the reader is able to learn and find inspiration through the experience of our two teachers, Nicholas Lodge and Janice Murfitt whose work is so lavishly and comprehensively illustrated throughout.

There is also the promise of even more to come in the second book which builds upon the knowledge gained in this volume, teaching sophisticated skills to a high standard of achievement. Meanwhile, I hope that you have many hours of enjoyment from the chapters that follow and find them a source of inspiration for years to come.

Deborah Gray.
Managing editor

Contents

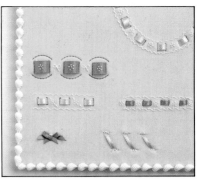
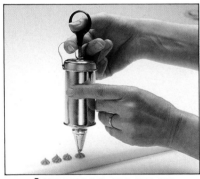

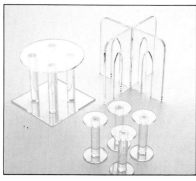

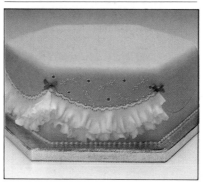

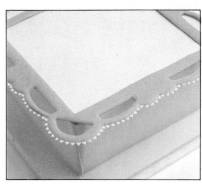

TULLE

MODELLING

LETTERING

NICHOLAS LODGE

Nicholas Lodge became interested in the art of sugarcraft at an early age, designing his first cake at the age of ten. After finishing school he studied at the National Bakery School in London where he was a distinguished student winning the prize for the best decoration student in his year.

Nicholas then worked as Principle Wedding Cake Designer for one of Britain's leading commercial cake decorating companies where he worked on commissions for many leading stores and hotels. At the age of twenty-one Nicholas became Tutorial Manager at a well-known cake decorating school where he taught at all levels, including instructing a large number of overseas students.

Today Nicholas teaches, lectures and demonstrates sugarcraft, as well as carrying out cake commissions and running his own cake decorating and floristry business. In his busy schedule he also finds time to travel extensively, lecturing and teaching in America, Australia, South Africa and several Far-Eastern countries. On his last visit to the Orient he was even commissioned to decorate a nine-and-a-half foot cake to celebrate the visit of the Prince and Princess of Wales to Japan. Nicholas is often assisted on trips by his wife, Sindy who is also a cake decorator.

In 1985 Nicholas wrote his first book for Merehurst Press, the highly successful, *Sugar Flowers.* Since then he has gone on to write *The Art of Sugarcraft – Pastillage and Sugar Moulding,* and in the same series, *Lace and Filigree.*

At the age of twenty-five Nicholas has already achieved a great deal in his career and has become one of the brightest lights in his field. However, his ambition now is to combine his interests and to run his own school of sugarcraft and floristry.

JANICE MURFITT

Janice Murfitt is the author of a whole library of cookery books, and has always been keenly interested in all aspects of cookery, particularly cake decorating and icing. An enthusiastic traveller, Janice has combined this interest with her love of cookery and is an avid collector of local recipes from a wide range of countries.

Janice started her career as a home economist in London, producing recipes, food for photography, advertising and television commercials and educational films on food.

For several years, Janice worked in the cookery department of a well known magazine, writing features, creating recipes and preparing food for photography. She now works as a freelance creative home economist and her skills are in great demand.

Janice Murfitt is married with two daughters.

How to use the Book

Text all skills and projects are fully explained in clear, easy-to-follow text which provides you with detailed information which is then supplemented by the step-by-step instructions and photographs.

Ingredients and measurements are given in metric, imperial and where appropriate, cups. Remember to use only one system of measurement at any one time.

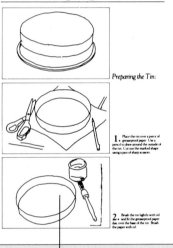

Step-by-step photography takes you through the skills covered in the book.

Numbered steps ensure that the sequence of photographs is apparent at a glance.

Equipment clear indications are given of the equipment necessary for each project so that you can have it to hand before starting work.

Colour photographs appear throughout the book and should be used as a reference to assist you with the fine detail of your own work.

Detailed captions are provided to accompany the step-by-step photography for additional clarity.

FOREWORD

We are very honoured to be asked to write a foreword for the book *The International School of Sugarcraft, Book 1* by Nicholas Lodge. We first heard of Nicholas on a previous trip and actually met him during our last tour of England. He escorted us to a Portsmouth cake decorating show and we saw his own exhibit which was outstanding.

Recently we caught up with him in Johannesburg where we were privileged to see him at work again. We attended two of his classes featuring royal icing techniques and were impressed with his command of the class and the high standard of work he demonstrated. He has had vast experience in many fields including marzipan, royal icing, moulded flowers, sugarpaste and chocolate.

We know that this talented young man will go a long way in the field of sugar art and wish him well with his books.

Marie Sykes and Patricia Simmons

Lesson 1

Equipment

Equipment

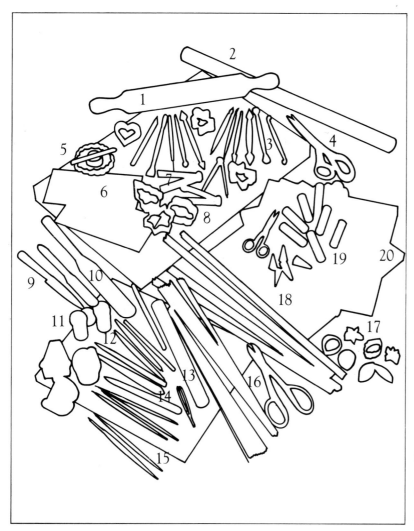

1. Rolling pin and worksurface
2. Greaseproof (waxed) paper
3. Metal modelling tools
4. Scissors
5. Garrett frill cutter
6. Smoothers
7. Crimpers
8. Selection of pastry and cookie cutters
9. Kitchen knife
10. Palette knives
11. Paste colours
12. Sugarcraft pens
13. Small non-stick rolling pin and board
14. Wooden modelling tools
15. Paintbrushes
16. Floristry wire and wire cutters
17. Flower cutters
18. Piping tubes
19. Petal dust
20. Cake boards and cards

Brushes

Use sable-hair brushes for the best effect and have several different sizes to hand.

Cake boards

These come in a wide variety of shapes and sizes designed to correspond with the various cake tins (pans) on the market. These are covered in greater detail in chapter (13)

Cocktail sticks

Used to add colouring paste to icing and in modelling work. Japanese birch are the best quality sticks that are available.

Colours

Dry dusting colours, paste colours and liquid food colouring are all needed for the various techniques covered in this and the companion volume.

Crimpers and leather embossing tools

Used for decorating sugarpaste and marzipan. See below for further details.

Cutters

A wide selection of cutters is useful. Flower, pastry, sweet (candy) and biscuit (cookie) cutters are used for making plaques and cutouts, while frills and flounces are made with Garrett cutters.

Dummies

Used for practice and competition work. See below for further details.

Electric mixer

Useful in cake preparation and for making royal icing.

Ball tools

A selection of different sizes are required although a glass-headed pin stuck into a piece of dowelling can be used in place of a small ball tool.

Bowls

A selection of various sizes, preferably glass, all clean and free of grease.

Florist's wire

You will need varying gauges for flower work, and modelling.

Icing bag stand

Not essential but keeps the worksurface clean and stops the tubes, once filled from drying out.

Knives

A good kitchen knife with a fine sharp blade is essential, you may also wish to use a scalpel for fine cutting and trimming work.

Measuring jug

The 500ml (1pint) is most useful.

Modelling tools

These may be bought from specialist suppliers although you will be able to improvise with various common household tools.

Moulds

Used in sugarcraft work and chocolate work and come in a wide variety of shapes and sizes for many different occasions.

Palette knife

Crank-handled and straight palette knives are used for lifting, smoothing and trimming.

Paper and card

Greaseproof (waxed) and silicone paper is used for icing bags and runouts. Card is used to make templates.

Dummy Cakes

There are three main types of dummy cake used for practising and for competition work. The polystyrene dummies come in a range of different shapes and sizes, they generally work well but are very light weight. This can be overcome by hollowing out the inside and filling with wall plaster or plaster of Paris. Royal icing is usually used to attach the dummy to the cake board, allow to dry for a few hours before coating. Alternatively, if the dummy is to be sugarpasted, stick to the board with clear piping jelly. Piping jelly may also be used to attach the paste to the dummy. When cleaning the dummy, remove from the board and soak in warm water, never attempt to cut the icing from the dummy with a sharp knife as this will damage the polystyrene.

Dummies can also be created from a stack of cake boards stuck together with royal icing or glue. Because of the ridges along the edges, this dummy type is most suitable for royal icing rather than paste. Board dummys cannot be washed but layers of practice coating may be built up.

Finally there is the wooden dummy. If you plan on doing a good deal of competition work or practising then it is worth investing in a good quality wooden dummy. These are suitable for all types of work and are easy to wash and reuse. Most dummies do have an attached wooden board which can be a disadvantage if you wish to practise collars or extension work but most dummies can be unscrewed and used separately using an ordinary cake-board.

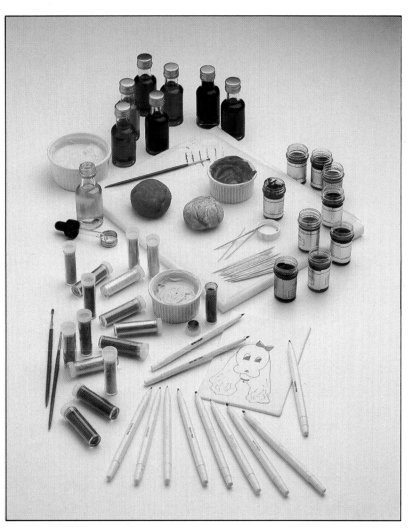

Piping tubes

Various sizes and shapes are available in both nickle plate and plastic. The former are more expensive but tend to be more accurate and defined.

Rolling pin

An extra long or non-stick pin is necessary and a smaller stainless steel or non-stick pin is useful for making plaques and for fine work.

Scissors

One good pair of large scissors and a pair of sharp fine bladed scissors are also required.

Scrapers

Plain and serrated plastic side scrapers are used for or putting royal icing on the sides of cakes.

Scriber

Fine lines are scratched or scribed onto the cake using a scriber.

Sieve

Keep a small fine mesh sieve for sieving icing sugar only.

Smoothers

These are used to smooth the surface of marzipanned or sugarpasted cakes although some people prefer to use their hands.

Spacers

These help to maintain uniform thickness when rolling out sugarpaste or marzipan.

Spatula

Plastic or rubber for use in cake and icing preparation and wooden for mixing royal icing.

Food Colouring

Food colouring comes in four main forms: powder, liquid, paste and pens.

Powder is mainly used as petal dust as for adding colour to flowers and frills. It can be used to colour the icing itself but the intensity is not so strong as with paste or liquid colouring so it is uneconomical to use in large quantities. However, it should be used for lace and filigree work as paste contains glycerine and liquid would make the icing too soft for fine work. Powders should also be used when colouring white chocolate as other types would cause it to thicken.

Liquid colourings are readily available but are less concentrated than paste consequently making sugarpaste more sticky and royal icing too soft if used in any quantity. Use for pastel shades only and use paste for dark colours.

Paste colours are generally the best to use for colouring royal icing or sugarpaste. Pastes are glycerine based and come in a good colour range. Use a cocktail stick to add the colour to the icing and use sparingly.

Sugarcraft pens are also available and are used for marking outlines, and writing on surfaces. They are used like a felt pen.

Straight edge
Used when flat icing the top of a cake with royal icing.

Tweezers
Use fine pointed tweezers with grooved ends.

Turntable
Preferably a quality turntable; a tilting one is best for some jobs.

Wooden dowelling
Used for pulled flower work and modelling.

Work surface
Melamine, non-stick plastic, marble or wooden surfaces are best. Be sure that they are thoroughly clean and grease-free.

Care of Equipment
Wash each piece of equipment thoroughly after use in warm, mild detergent taking care to ensure that all items are free of grease. Rinse before drying. Store in a dry, dust-free environment, rewash before use if necessary.

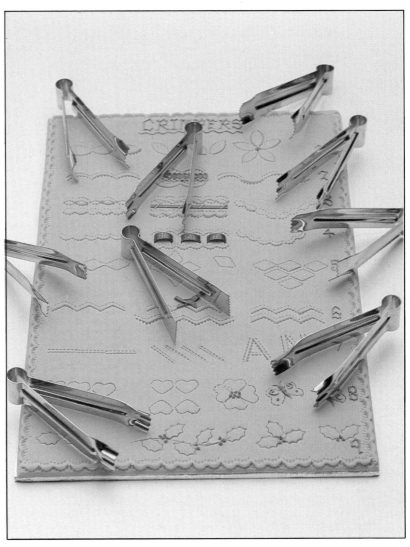

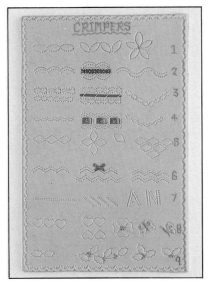

Crimper Plaque 2
The numbers along the edge of the plaque relate to the particular set of crimpers shown above.

No. 1 Single open scallop
No. 2 Single closed scallop
No. 3 Double open scallop
No. 4 Double closed scallop
No. 5 Diamond
No. 6 Chevron
No. 7 Straight edge
No. 8 Heart
No. 9 Holly

Crimper Plaque 1
The plaque shows a full set of crimpers with their corresponding effects. Crimpers are a quick and versatile method of decoration for marzipanned and sugarpasted surfaces. Crimping must always be worked on soft paste so is generally worked as soon as the cake is covered. When using crimpers dip in cornflour (cornstarch) to prevent them sticking to the paste while working. Pinch the crimper slightly so the edges are about 5mm (¼in) from the closed position, place on the sugarpaste surface and bring your thumb and first finger together. Squeeze the crimper to create the desired effect.

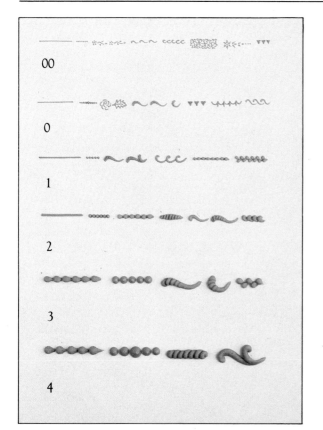

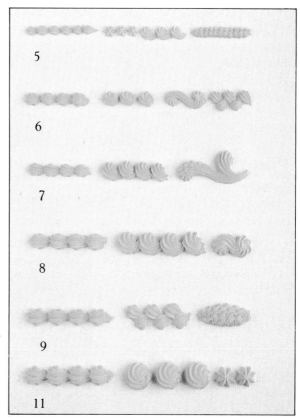

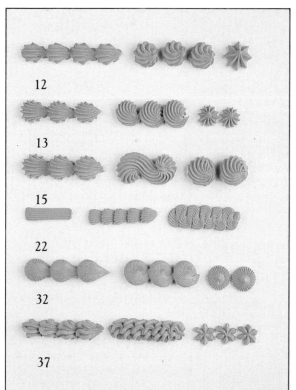

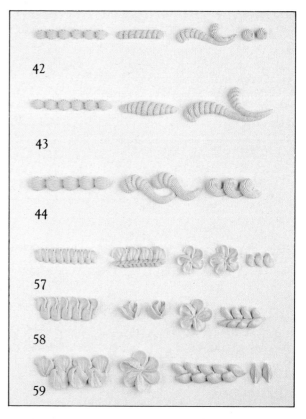

Sponge Cakes

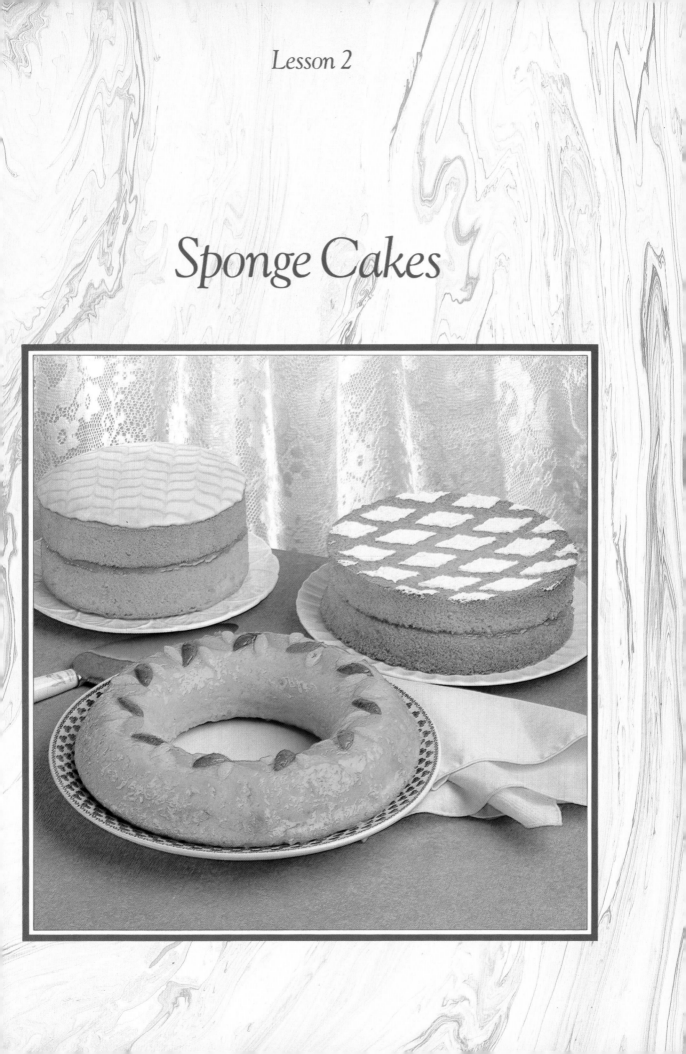

Basic Sponge Cake

This is a traditional sponge cake made by creaming together the butter and sugar to incorporate the air. The result is very similar to the one-bowl sponge but the texture is slightly firmer, making it easier to ice and decorate.

Place the butter or margarine and sugar in a mixing bowl. Mix together with a wooden spoon, then beat for 2 to 3 minutes until light and fluffy. Alternatively, use an electric mixer for about 1 minute.

Add the eggs a little at a time, beating well after each addition, until all the egg has been incorporated and the mixture is soft and glossy. If it looks slightly curdled, beat in 15-30ml (1-2 tablespoons) of flour.

Sift the flour into the bowl and add flavourings if wished. Using a spatula or a large spoon, carefully fold in the flour, cutting through and turning the mixture until all the flour has been incorporated into the batter.

Place the mixture into the prepared greased and lined tin; smooth the top with a spatula and give the tin a sharp tap to remove any air pockets and to level the mixture.

Place the cake mixture in the centre of a pre-heated oven 160°C (325°F/Gas 3) for the specified cooking time (see Basic Sponge chart). Test the cake by pressing the centre with the fingers. The cake should be golden brown and feel firm and springy when cooked.

Loosen the edges with a palette knife, invert onto a cooling rack and remove the lining paper. Turn the cake the right way up and leave until cold completely.

INGREDIENTS
See Basic Sponge Chart page 33

Flavourings for a 2-egg quantity of Basic Sponge Cake (increase the amounts for larger quantities of cake mixture):
15ml (1 tablespoon) cocoa blended with 15ml (1 tablespoon) boiling water
10ml (2 teaspoons) instant coffee blended with 5ml (1 teaspoon) boiling water
5-10ml (1-2 teaspoons) finely grated orange, lemon or lime rind
2.5ml (½ teaspoon) vanilla, almond or peppermint essence (extract) 25g (1oz/1 tablespoon) chocolate dots (chips) or grated chocolate
50g (2oz/¼ cup) glacé (candied) cherries, chopped

Making a Basic Creamed Sponge Cake

Preparing the Tin

1. Place the tin over a piece of greaseproof paper. Use a pencil to draw around the outside of the tin. Cut out the marked shape using a pair of sharp scissors.

2. Brush the tin lightly with oil and fit the greaseproof paper disc over the base of the tin. Brush the paper with oil.

3. Cream together the butter and sugar in a mixing bowl using a wooden spoon.

4. Beat the mixture until light and fluffy.

5. Add the eggs a little at a time, beating well after each addition.

6. Beat until smooth and glossy.

7. Sift the flour into the bowl.

8. Using a spatula or metal spoon to fold the flour carefully into the mixture until all the flour is incorporated.

9. Place the mixture into the tin and spread evenly using a small palette knife.

10. Mixture level, ready to bake.

11. Loosen the edge of the cake away from the tin using a small palette knife.

12. Turn the cake out onto a cooling rack.

13. Carefully peel off the lining paper.

14. Invert the cake and cool on the wire rack.

Whisked Sponge Cake

A light, fat-free sponge suitable for making into Swiss rolls (jelly rolls), small and large iced and decorated sponge and novelty cakes.

Place the eggs and sugar in a heat-proof bowl over a saucepan of hot but not boiling water. Whisk the mixture until thick and pale. Remove the bowl from the saucepan and continue whisking until, when lifted, the whisk leaves a trail of mixture on the surface.

Sift the flour and baking powder onto the surface of the mixture and add any flavourings. Using a spatula or a large spoon, carefully fold in the flour, cutting through and turning the mixture until all the flour has been incorporated.

Pour the mixture into the prepared greased and lined tin (see chart) and gently level the top with a spatula.

Place the cake in the centre of a pre-heated oven 180°C (350°F/Gas 4) for the specified cooking time (see chart). Test the cake by pressing the centre with the fingers. The cake should be golden brown feel firm and springy when cooked.

Loosen the edges with a palette knife and invert onto a cooling rack. Carefully remove the lining paper, turn the cake the right way up and leave until cold.

INGREDIENTS

See Whisked Sponge Cake Chart page 33

Flavouring for a 2-egg quantity of Whisked Sponge Cake (increase the amounts for larger quantities of cake mixture)
Chocolate: replace 15g (½oz/2 tablespoons) flour with cocoa powder
Coffee: add 10ml (2 teaspoons) instant coffee powder to the flour
Citrus: add 5ml (1 teaspoon) grated orange, lemon or lime rind
Nut: replace 25g (1oz/¼ cup) flour with finely ground nuts

Making a Swiss Roll

Preparing the Tin

1. Place the tin in the centre of a piece of greaseproof paper, 2.5cm (1in) larger all round than the tin. Cut from the corner of the paper to the corner of the tin using a pair of sharp scissors.

2. Lightly brush the tin with oil and fit the paper into the tin. Brush the paper lightly with oil.

3. Whisk the eggs and sugar in a bowl over a saucepan of hot water until light and thick.

4. Lift the whisk to show a trail on the surface.

5. Sift the flour onto the surface of the mixture.

6. Fold the flour carefully into the mixture.

7. Spread the mixture carefully into the corners of the tin.

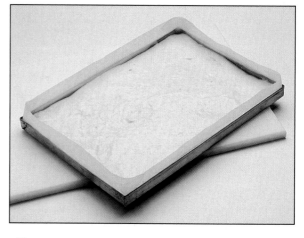

8. Level mixture in the tin ready to bake.

9. Sprinkle a piece of greaseproof paper with caster (superfine) sugar.

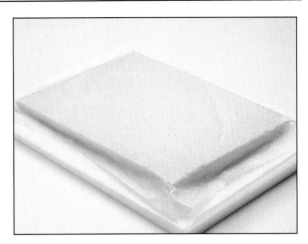

10. Invert the cake on to the sugared paper.

11. Carefully peel off the lining paper.

12. Trim 5mm (¼in) off each side of the cake using a sharp knife.

13. Spread the trimmed cake evenly with warmed apricot jam.

14. Roll the cake towards you into a firm roll starting with the aid of the paper, from the short edge.

One-Bowl Sponge Cake

A quick and easy cake to make simply by mixing the ingredients together in one bowl. Different flavourings can be added to give variety. The mixture may be cooked in many different tin shapes and sizes (see chart).

Place the flour, baking powder, sugar, margarine and eggs into a mixing bowl. Mix together with a wooden spoon, then beat for 2 to 3 minutes until smooth and glossy. Alternatively, use an electric mixer and beat for 1 minute only. Add any flavourings if wished and mix until well blended.

Place the mixture into the prepared greased and lined tin; smooth the top with a spatula and give the tin a sharp tap to remove any air pockets and to level the mixture.

Place the cake mixture in the centre of a pre-heated oven 160°C (325°F/Gas 3) for the specified cooking time (see chart). Test the cake by pressing the centre with the fingers. The cake should be golden brown and feel firm and springy when cooked.

Loosen the edges with a palette knife, invert onto a cooling rack and remove the lining paper. Turn the cake the right way up and leave until completely cold.

INGREDIENTS

See One-Bowl Sponge Cake Chart page 33

Flavourings for a 2-egg quantity of One-Bowl Sponge Cake (increase the amounts for larger quantities of cake mixture)
15ml (1 tablespoon) cocoa blended with 15ml (1 tablespoon) boiling water
10ml (2 teaspoons) instant coffee blended with 5ml (1 teaspoon) boiling water
5-10ml (1-2 teaspoons) finely grated orange, lemon or lime rind
2.5ml (½ teaspoon) vanilla, almond or peppermint essence (extract) 25g (1oz/1 tablespoon) chocolate dots (chips) or grated chocolate
50g (2oz/¼ cup) glacé (candied) cherries, chopped

Genoese Sponge Cake

A rich sponge cake made with melted butter which gives a moist, light texture. It will cut well into different shapes for small, large or novelty cakes, and is easy to ice.

Place the eggs and sugar in a heatproof bowl. Put the bowl over a saucepan of hot, but not boiling water and whisk immediately. Whisk until thick and pale, for about 3 to 4 minutes. Remove the bowl from the saucepan and continue whisking until, when the whisk is lifted, the mixture leaves a trail on the surface.

Sift the flour onto the surface of the mixture and add any flavourings if desired. Pour the melted butter around the edge of the mixture.

Using a spatula or large spoon, carefully fold in the flour and butter, cutting through and turning the mixture gently until all the flour has been incorporated.

Pour the mixture into the prepared greased and lined tin (see chart) and gently level the top with a spatula. Place the cake mixture in the centre of a pre-heated oven 180°C (350°F/ Gas 4) for the specified cooking time (see chart). Test the cake by pressing the centre with the fingers. The cake should be golden brown and feel firm and springy when cooked.

Loosen the edges with a palette knife and invert onto a cooling rack. Carefully remove the lining paper, turn the cake the right way up and leave until cold.

INGREDIENTS

See Genoese Sponge Cake Chart page 34

Flavourings for a 2-egg quantity of Genoese Sponge Cake (increase the amounts for larger quantities of cake mixture)
Chocolate: replace 15g (½oz/2 tablespoons) flour with cocoa powder
Coffee: add 10ml (2 teaspoons) instant coffee powder to the flour
Citrus: add 5ml (1 teaspoon) grated orange, lemon or lime rind
Nut: replace 25g (1oz/¼ cup) flour with finely ground nuts

Quick Madeira Cake

A good, plain cake which can be made as an alternative to a light or rich fruit cake. It is firm and moist and makes a good base for icing and decorating.

Place the flour, baking powder, sugar, margarine, eggs and milk into a mixing bowl. Mix together with a wooden spoon, then beat for 2 to 3 minutes until smooth and glossy. Alternatively, use an electric mixer and beat for 1 minute only. Add any flavourings if wished and mix until well blended.

Place the mixture into the prepared greased and lined tin (see chart); smooth the top with a spatula and give the tin a sharp tap to remove any air pockets and to level the top.

Place the cake mixture in the centre of a pre-heated oven 160°C (325°F/Gas 3) for the specified cooking time (see chart). Test the

cake by pressing the centre with the fingers. The cake should be golden brown.

Loosen the edges with a palette knife, invert onto a cooling rack and remove the lining paper. Turn the cake the right way up and leave until completely cold.

INGREDIENTS

see Quick Madeira Cake Chart page 33

Flavourings for a 3-egg quantity of Madeira Cake (increase the amounts for larger quantities of cake mixture)
Cherry: 185g (6oz/¾ cup) glacé (candied) cherries, halved
Coconut: 60g (2oz/⅔ cup) dessicated (shredded) coconut
Nut: replace 125g (4oz/1 cup) flour with ground almonds, hazelnuts, walnuts or pecan nuts
Citrus: replace milk with lemon, orange or lime juice and 5ml (1 teaspoon) of grated lemon, orange or lime rind

American Sponge Cake

Thistle white sponge cake makes a good base for a celebration cake; it can be marzipanned, iced and decorated.

For Ingredients see American Sponge Cake Chart page 34

Place the butter and sugar in a mixing bowl. Mix together with a wooden spoon, then beat for 2 to 3 minutes until light and fluffy. Alternatively, use an electric mixer for 1 minute.

Sift together the flour and baking powder. Gradually add the flour to the mixture with the water, beating well after each addition, until all the flour and water have been fully incorporated, to form a smooth lump-free batter.

Place the egg whites in a clean, grease-free bowl and whisk until stiff, but not dry. Add one-third of the egg whites to the mixture. Using a spatula or a large metal spoon, carefully fold in the egg whites, cutting through and turning the mixture until all the egg whites have been incorporated. Repeat this process with the remaining egg whites.

Pour the mixture into the prepared greased and lined tin (see chart) and gently level the top with a spatula. Place the cake mixture in the centre of a pre-heated oven 180°C (350°F/ Gas 4) for the specified cooking time (see chart). Test the cake by pressing the centre with the fingers. The cake should be golden brown and feel firm and springy when cooked.

Loosen the edges with a palette knife and invert onto a cooling rack. Carefully remove the lining paper, turn the cake the right way up and leave until cold.

Simple Decorations

There are many simple ways in which a basic sponge cake can be decorated without spending a lot of time. It is always a pleasure to add a finishing touch to a cake to turn it into something a little more special.

Icing (confectioner's) sugar is one ingredient which, when used carefully, can transform the appearance of a cake. Simply dredging the surface with icing sugar makes a sponge cake more appealing. Try placing a patterned doily on top of a cake, or arranging 1cm (½in) strips of paper in lines or a lattice pattern on top of the cake; then dredge thickly with icing sugar. Carefully remove the doily or paper strips, revealing the pattern, in sugar. This looks most effective on a chocolate or coffee cake.

Fruit rinds cut into shapes using tiny cutters make an effective edible decoration. Cut thin strips of lemon, orange or lime rind from the fruits, taking care not to include the white pith. Using tiny aspic or cocktail cutters, cut out various shapes. Arrange these shapes on glacé-icing or cakes iced with buttercream to form flowers, stems and leaves, or just as a continuous border using the same shape but different coloured rinds.

Flowers seem a natural decoration to go on a cake; tiny fresh flowers positioned at the last minute look so pretty. Also attractive are sugar-frosted flowers, which are preserved with egg white and sugar; they will last for several weeks once they are completely dry.

To sugar-frost flowers, ensure they are fresh and dry and trim the stems to the length required. Pull the petals apart if you wish to frost each one of them separately.

Place some caster (superfine) sugar in a shallow bowl. Using a fine paint brush, paint each petal on both sides with egg white which has been lightly beaten. Brush the centre and stem, then carefully spoon over the sugar to coat evenly.

Place the flowers on a cooling rack covered with kitchen paper and leave in a warm, dry place until the flowers are completely dry and set hard.

Store in a box lined with kitchen paper for up to three weeks.

Glacé Icing

This icing is simply made from icing (confectioner's) sugar and boiling water, see page 83 for recipe. Pour over the top of the cake. Spread evenly to the edge and decorate with fruit rinds, cherries, angelica, nuts or flowers.

Feather icing is very pretty; working with a white and coloured glacé icing. Place the coloured icing into a paper piping bag and snip the point off the end. Spread the top of the cake evenly with white icing and quickly pipe evenly spaced lines of coloured icing across the top of the white icing.

Draw a cocktail stick backwards and forwards through the icing across the lines to form a feather design. Leave to set.

Purchased decorations are instant decorations and, chosen carefully, can make a pretty finish to a cake. Angelica can be cut into stems, leaves and diamond shapes. Glacé cherries in various colours can be cut in half or sliced into rings or into thin wedges and arranged as petal shapes for flowers. Sugar flowers, jelly diamonds, (gumdrops) crystallized flower petals all make attractive decorations on top of icing swirls or as a border design. Coloured dragées, sugared mimosa balls, hundreds and thousands (sprinkles), coloured sugar

strands make quick, colourful coatings, toppings and designs.

For children's cakes, sweets (candies) are always a favourite;

white and chocolate buttons, coloured (jelly) beans and liquorice sweets can all be used for simple finishes.

Basic Sponge and One-Bowl Sponge Chart

Tin (Pan) Sizes	17.5cm (7in) shallow square tin 20cm (8in) round sandwich (shallow) tin	1kg (2lb) loaf tin 22.5cm (9in) ring mould (tube pan)	940ml (30fl oz/3¾ cups) pudding basin or (bowl) or mould	Two 17.5cm (7in) shallow square tins Two 20cm (8in) sandwich (shallow) tins	1 litre (32fl oz/4 cups) pudding basin (bowl) 17.5cm (7in) mould	1kg (2lb) loaf tin 27.5cm x 17.5cm (11in x 7in) oblong tin	Two 20cm (8in) round sandwich (shallow) tins Two 22.5cm (9in) round sandwich (shallow) tins	22.5cm (9in) deep round or square cake tin
Self-raising Flour	125g (4oz/1 cup)	125g (4oz/1 cup)	125g (4oz/1 cup)	185g (6oz/1½ cups)	185g (6oz/1½ cups)	185g (6oz/1½ cups)	250g (8oz/2 cups)	250g (8oz/2 cups)
Baking Powder	5ml 1 teaspoon	5ml 1 teaspoon	5ml 1 teaspoon	7.5ml 1½ teaspoons	7.5ml 1½ teaspoons	7.5ml 1½ teaspoons	10ml 2 teaspoons	10ml 2 teaspoons
Caster (superfine) Sugar	125g (4oz/½ cup)	125g (4oz/½ cup)	125g (4oz/½ cup)	185g (6oz/¾ cup)	185g (6oz/¾ cup)	185g (6oz/¾ cup)	250g (8oz/1 cup)	250g (8oz/1 cup)
Soft Margarine	125g (4oz/½ cup)	125g (4oz/½ cup)	125g (4oz/½ cup)	185g (6oz/¾ cup)	185g (6oz/¾ cup)	185g (6oz/¾ cup)	250g (8oz/1 cup)	250g (8oz/1 cup)
Medium Eggs	2	2	2	3	3	3	4	4
Approximate Cooking Time	35 to 40 minutes	30 to 35 minutes	50 to 55 minutes	30 to 35 minutes	60 to 70 minutes	45 to 55 minutes	35 to 40 minutes	55 to 65 minutes

Whisked Sponge Chart

Tin (pan) Sizes	27.5cm x 17.5cm (11in x 7in) Swiss (Jelly) roll tin	17.5cm (7in) shallow square tin 20cm (8in) round sandwich (shallow) tin	32.5cm x 22.5cm (13in x 9in) Swiss (jelly) roll tin Two 17.5cm (7in) shallow square tins	20cm (8in) round cake tin	Two 20cm (8in) round sandwich (shallow) tins Two 17.5cm (7in) shallow square tins	17.5cm (7in) square cake tin
Medium Eggs	2	2	3	3	4	4
Caster (superfine) Sugar	50g (2oz/¼ cup)	50g (2oz/¼ cup)	90g (3oz/⅓ cup)	90g (3oz/⅓ cup)	125g (4oz/½ cup)	125g (4oz/½ cup)
Plain (all-purpose) Flour	50g (2oz/½ cup)	50g (2oz/½ cup)	90g 3oz/¾ cup)	90g (3oz/¾ cup)	125g (4oz/1 cup)	125g (4oz/1 cup)
Baking Powder	2.5ml (½ teaspoon)	2.5ml (½ teaspoon)	2.5ml (½ teaspoon)	2.5ml (½ teaspoon)	2.5ml (½ teaspoon)	2.5ml (½ teaspoon)
Approximate Cooking Time	10 to 15 minutes	20 to 25 minutes	10 to 15 minutes	30 to 35 minutes	20 to 25 minutes	30 to 35 minutes

Quick Madeira Chart

Tin (pan) Sizes	15.5cm (6in) square 17.5cm (7in) round	17.5cm (7in) square 20cm (8in) round	20cm (8in) square 22.5cm (9in) round	22.5cm (9in) square 25cm (10in) round
Plain (all-purpose) Flour	250g (8oz/2 cups)	375g (12oz/3 cups)	500g (1lb/4 cups)	560g (1lb 2oz/4¼ cups)
Baking Powder	5ml (1 teaspoon)	7.5ml (1½ teaspoons)	10ml (2 teaspoons)	12.5ml (2½ teaspoons)
Caster (superfine) Sugar	185g (6oz/¾ cup)	315g (10oz/1¼ cups)	440g (14oz/1¾ cups)	500g (1lb/2 cups)
Soft Margarine	185g (6oz/¾ cup)	315g (10oz/1¼ cups)	440g (14oz/1¾ cups)	500g (1lb/2 cups)
Medium Eggs	3	5	7	8
Milk or Citrus Juice	30ml (2 tablespoons)	45ml (3 tablespoons)	52.5ml (3½ tablespoons)	60ml (4 tablespoons)
Approximate Cooking Time	1¼ to 1½ hours	1½ to 1¾ hours	1¾ to 2 hours	1¾ to 2 hours

Genoese Sponge Chart

Cake Tin (pan) Sizes	32.5cm x 22.5cm (13in x 9in) Two 17.5cm (7in) square Two 20cm (8in) round sandwich	Two 20cm (8in) shallow square Two 22.5cm (9in) round sandwich (shallow)	22.5cm (9in) deep square 25cm (10in) deep round
Medium Eggs	4	6	8
Caster (superfine) Sugar	125g (4oz/½ cup)	185g (6oz/¾ cup)	250g (8oz/1 cup)
Plain (all-purpose) Flour	125g (4oz/1 cup)	185g (6oz/1½ cups)	250g (8oz/2 cups)
Unsalted (sweet) Butter, melted	50g (2oz/¼ cup)	90g (3oz/⅓ cup)	125g (4oz/½ cup)
Approximate Cooking Time	15 minutes to 20 minutes	25 to 30 minutes	35 to 40 minutes

American Sponge Chart

Tin (pan) Sizes	17.5cm (7in) square 20cm (8in) round 22.5cm (9in) ring (tube) tin	20cm (8in) square 22.5cm (9in) round	22.5cm (9in) square 25cm (10in) round
Butter, softened	125g (4oz/½ cup)	250g (8oz/1 cup)	375g (12oz/1½ cups)
Caster (superfine) Sugar	185g (6oz/¾ cup)	375g (12oz/1¼ cups)	560g (1lb 2oz/2 cups)
Plain (all-purpose) Flour	220g (7oz/1¾ cups)	440g (14oz/3½ cups)	655g (1lb 5oz/5¼ cups)
Baking Powder	10ml (2 teaspoons)	20ml (4 teaspoons)	30ml (6 teaspoons)
Water	125ml (4fl oz/½ cup)	250ml (8fl oz/1 cup)	375ml (12fl oz/1½ cups)
Vanilla Essence (extract)	2.5ml (½ teaspoon)	5 ml (1 teaspoon)	7.5ml (1½ teaspoon)
Medium Egg Whites	4	8	12
Approximate Cooking Time	35 to 45 minutes	60 to 65 minutes	60 to 65 minutes

Lesson 3

Fruit Cakes

Rich Fruit Cake

This recipe makes a very moist, rich cake suitable for any celebration. The cake can be made in stages, if time is short or if you are making more than one cake, see page 46 for chart of ingredients.

The fruit may be prepared and soaked overnight and the cake made the following day. Once the mixture is in the tin, the surface may be covered with cling film and the cake stored in a cool place overnight if cooking is not possible on the day. The quantities have been carefully worked out so that the depth of each cake is the same. This is important when making tiers for a wedding cake, as they must all be the same depth.

Place in a large mixing bowl the raisins, sultanas, currants, apricots, glacé cherries, mixed peel, nuts, lemon rind and juice, brandy, whisky or sherry.

Mix all the ingredients together until well blended, then cover the bowl with cling film. This mixture of fruit can be left overnight if required.

In another mixing bowl place the flour, ground almonds, mixed spice, sugar, butter, treacle and eggs.

Mix together with a wooden spoon, then beat for 2 to 3 minutes

until smooth and glossy, or beat for 1 to 2 minutes using an electric mixer or food processor.

Place the mixed fruit into the bowl with the cake mixture. Stir gently until all the fruit has been mixed into the cake mixture.

Spoon the mixture carefully into the prepared tin and spread evenly over the base and into the corners. Give the tin a few sharp bangs to level the mixture and to remove any air pockets. Smooth the surface with the back of a metal spoon dipped in hot water, making a slight depression in the centre. The cake surface may be covered with cling film and left overnight in a cool place if required.

Place the cake in the centre of a pre-heated oven 140°C (275°F/Gas 1) for the specified cooking time (see chart page 46).

Test the cake to see if it is cooked 15 minutes before the end of the cooking time. If cooked, the cake should feel firm and when a fine

skewer or cocktail stick is inserted into the centre, it should come out quite clean.

If the cake is not cooked, re-test it at 15 minute intervals. Remove the cake from the oven and allow it to cool in the tin.

Turn the cake out of the tin but do not remove the lining paper as it helps to keep the cake moist. Spoon another half quantity of brandy, whisky or sherry according to the quantities used in the chart, over the top of the cake and wrap in double thickness foil.

Store the cake in a cool, dry place on its base with the top uppermost for a week. Unwrap the cake and spoon over the remaining brandy, whisky or sherry (unless the cake is to be stored for three months in which case add the liquid a little at a time at monthly intervals). Re-wrap well and invert the cake and store it upsidedown to keep the top flat. The cake will store for up to 3 months.

Making a Rich Fruit Cake

1. Place all the dried fruits into a large mixing bowl.

2. Add the lemon rind juice and stir in the brandy, whisky, sherry if desired until evenly mixed, and set aside.

3. Place the remaining ingredients (sugar, flour, ground almonds, mixed spice, treacle (molasses), butter) into another bowl ready to add the eggs.

4. Stir all the ingredients together using a wooden spoon until mixed.

5. Beat the mixture together until well mixed, smooth and glossy.

6. Add the mixed fruit to the cake mixture.

7. Stir the fruit into the mixture.

8. Place the mixture in the prepared tin. Smooth the top of the cake mixture with the back of a wet metal spoon. Bake.

9. Cool the cooked cake in the tin.

10. Turn out the cold fruit
cake onto a wire rack.

11. Wrap the cake, with the
lining paper on, in foil
ready to store.

12. Unwrap the foil. Remove
the lining paper from the
fruit cake.

Light Fruit Cake

This is a very light, moist fruit cake. As there is less fruit in the cake, it has a tendency to dome during cooking, so make a deep depression in the centre before putting in the oven. The cake will keep for up to 4 weeks, see chart of ingredients page 44.

Prepare the required size deep cake tin according to the chart page 44.

Place in a large mixing bowl the mixed dried fruit, cherries, almonds, orange rind, and sherry. Mix all the ingredients together until well blended. In another mixing bowl, place the flour, mixed spice, sugar, butter or margarine and eggs.

Mix together with a wooden spoon until smooth and glossy, or beat for 1 to 2 minutes with an electric mixer or food processor.

Place the mixed fruit in the bowl with the cake mixture, stir gently until all the fruit has been mixed evenly into the cake mixture.

Spoon the mixture into the prepared cake tin and spread evenly over the base and into the corners. Give the tin a few sharp bangs to level the mixture and remove any air pockets. Smooth the surface with the back of a metal spoon, making a fairly deep depression in the centre.

Bake in a pre-heated oven 140°C

(275°F/Gas 1), following the chart cooking time guide. Test the cake 15 minutes before the end of the given cooking time. If cooked, a fine skewer or cocktail stick inserted into the centre of the cake will come out clean. If the cake is not cooked, re-test at 15 minute intervals.

Leave to cool in the tin, turn out and leave the lining paper on to ensure the cake keeps moist. Wrap in foil and store in a cool place for up to 4 weeks.

Glacé Fruit Cake

T his recipe makes a light-coloured cake with a moist texture which is due to the addition of ground almonds to the mixture. The cake will store well for several weeks and may be marzipanned and iced, or left plain.

Prepare the cake tin. Sift the flour and baking powder into a bowl, add the ground almonds, sugar, butter and eggs. Mix together with a wooden spoon and beat for 2 to 3 minutes until smooth and glossy, or beat for 1 to 2 minutes using an electric mixer or food processor.

Add the fruit and nuts to the mixture and stir gently until well mixed. Spoon the mixture into the prepared tin and spread evenly over the base and into the corners. Give a few sharp bangs to level the mixture and make a slight depression in the centre of the cake.

Bake in the centre of a pre-heated oven 140°C (275°F/Gas 1) for about 2¼ to 2½ hours. Test the cake by pressing the centre with the fingers. The cake should feel firm and springy when cooked. Leave to cool in the tin, then turn out and wrap the cake in foil and store in a cool place for up to one week before decorating.

Makes one 20cm (8in) square cake or a 22.5cm (9in) round cake.

Ingredients
375g (12oz/3 cups) plain (all-purpose) flour
5ml (1 teaspoon) baking powder
185g (6oz/1½ cups) ground almonds
375g (12oz/3 cups) caster (superfine) sugar
375g (12oz/3 cups) butter, softened
4 large eggs
375g (12oz/3 cups) chopped mixed glacé fruits
125g (4oz/1 cup) chopped Brazil nuts

Wheaten Fruit Cake

This wholesome fruit cake is made from a mixture of dried fruits, honey and wholewheat flour. It is easy to make and produces a moist cake which will keep for several weeks. Decorate it with fruit and nuts, or cover it with marzipan and icing.

Prepare the tin. Place the butter, honey and orange juice into a large saucepan. Heat gently until the butter has melted, then bring to the boil. Remove the saucepan from the heat then stir in the fruit until well mixed, then leave until lukewarm.

Place the flour, mixed spice and eggs into a large mixing bowl. Stir the bicarbonate of soda quickly into the fruit mixture, then add to the flour mixture in the bowl.

Mix together with a wooden spoon, then stir until well mixed. Spoon the mixture into the prepared tin and spread evenly over the base and into the corners. Give a few sharp bangs to level the mixture and make a slight depression in the centre.

Bake in the centre of a pre-heated oven 140°C (275°F/Gas 1) for about 2 hours. Test the cake 15 minutes from the end of the cooking time. When cooked, a fine skewer or cocktail stick inserted into the centre of the cake will come out clean. If the cake is not cooked, re-test at 15 minute intervals. Leave to cool in the tin, then turn out and wrap in foil for up to 2 weeks.

Makes one 17.5cm (7in) square cake or a 20cm (8in) round cake.

INGREDIENTS

125g (4oz/1 cup) butter
60ml (4 tablespoons) clear honey
250ml (8fl oz/1 cup) orange juice
375g (12oz/3 cups)
chopped dried apricots
250g (8oz/1½ cups)
chopped dried figs
250g (8oz/1½ cups)
chopped stoned dates
315g (10oz/1¾ cups) raisins
375g (12oz/3 cups) 85%
wholewheat plain flour
10ml (2 teaspoons)
ground mixed spice
4ml (¾ teaspoon) bicarbonate of
soda (baking soda)
2 eggs, beaten

Preparing a Deep Tin

For rich fruit cakes, use good quality fixed-based deep cake tins (pans). Ensure you have the correct-sized tin for the quantity of cake mixture as this will affect the depth and cooking time of the cake. Always measure the tin across the base, not the top.

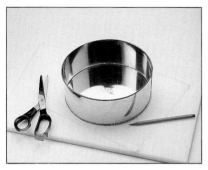

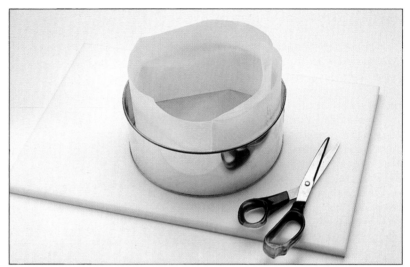

Double-line the inside of the tin with greaseproof or non-stick silicone baking paper and the outside with double-thickness brown paper. Stand the tin on a baking sheet lined with 3 or 4 thicknesses of brown paper. This prevents the side and base of the cake from being overcooked.

Place the tin on double-thickness greaseproof or non-stick silicone baking paper and draw around the base. Cut out the marked shape with a pair of scissors.

Cut a strip of double-thickness greaseproof or non-stick paper long enough to wrap around the outside of the tin with a small overlap and to stand 2.5cm (1in) above the top of the tin.

Brush the base and sides of the tin with melted fat or oil. Place the cut-out shape in the base of the tin and smooth out the creases.

Place the double strip of paper inside the tin, pressing well against the sides and making sharp creases where it fits into corners.

Brush the base and side paper well with melted fat or oil. Place a double-thickness strip of brown paper around the outside of the tin and tie securely with string.

Line a baking sheet with 3 or 4 layers of brown paper and stand the tin on top.

Decorating Ideas

Rich fruit cakes which are full of flavour are often enjoyed without marzipan and icing. Included in this section is a very rich fruit cake suitable for all celebration cakes. The light fruit cake is ideal for an everyday fruit cake as it is less expensive to make, and

Here are some simple decorations to give these cakes the finishing touches they deserve.

Apricot glaze brushed generously over the top of any fruit cake gives the top a glossy finish; when brushed over fruit or nut toppings it keeps them secure and moist.

Try arranging a variety of nuts over the top of the cake: a mixture of Brazil nuts, walnuts, almonds, pecan and hazelnuts. Brush the top of the cake before and after the nuts are applied.

Glacé fruits make a colourful and festive decoration; buy the pieces of fruit individually, or an assortment in a box: cherries in a variety of colours, pineapple slices, peaches, plums, pears, nectarines. Slice them thinly and arrange in rows across the top of the cake, brushing with apricot glaze before and after decorating.

The wheaten fruit cake lends itself to a topping of chopped apricots, figs and nuts drizzled with honey, or covered with raw sugar marzipan cutouts.

Purchased decorations provide the quickest and easiest way of decorating a fruit cake which has been already covered in marzipan and icing. They are available as seasonal decorations

and every kind of celebration occasion you can think of. Used sparingly and with a little thought, they can add colour and design to a cake. Ribbons of all shades, textures and width also look pretty around the outside of a cake, or tied into tiny bows or loops. Teamed up with fresh flowers, this is a simple way to decorate a cake.
(See photographs on page 35 and 45 for decorating ideas)

Light Fruit Cake Chart

Cake Tin (pan) Size	17.5cm (7in) square 20cm (8in) round	20cm (8in) square 22.5cm (9in) round	22.5cm (9in) square 25cm (10in) round
Mixed Dried Fruit	500g (1lb/3 cups)	750g (1½lb/4½ cups)	1kg (2lb/6 cups)
Glacé (candied) Cherries, quartered	90g (3oz/⅓ cup)	125g (4oz/½ cup)	185g (6oz/¾ cup)
Flaked Almonds	60g (2oz/½ cup)	90g (3oz/¾ cup)	125g (4oz/1 cup)
Orange Rind, coarsely grated	10ml (2 teaspoons)	15ml (3 teaspoons)	20ml (4 teaspoons)
Orange Juice	30ml (2 tablespoons)	45ml (3 tablespoons)	60ml (4 tablespoons)
Sherry	30ml (2 tablespoons)	45ml (3 tablespoons)	60ml (4 tablespoons)
Plain (all-purpose) Flour	375g (12oz/3 cups)	500g (1lb/4 cups)	625g (1¼lb/5 cups)
Ground Mixed Spice	10ml (2 teaspoons)	15ml (3 teaspoons)	20ml (4 teaspoons)
Soft light brown Sugar	315g (10oz/1¼ cups)	440g (14oz/1¾ cups)	530g (1lb 1oz/2⅓ cups)
Butter or Margarine, softened	315g (10oz/1¼ cups)	440g (14oz/1¾ cups)	530g (1lb 1oz/2⅓ cups)
Medium eggs	4	5	6
Approximate Cooking Time	2¾ to 3¼ hours	3¼ to 3¾ hours	3½ to 4 hours

it can also replace the rich cake if preferred. If you prefer a lighter cake, the glacé fruit cake is ideal – light in colour and texture – and for the health conscious, there is the wheaten fruit cake, rich in mixed dried fruits, wholemeal flour and honey.

Storing Fruit Cakes

Leave the lining paper on the cakes, then wrap in a double layer of foil, waxed paper or greaseproof paper, and store in a cool, dry place. Never seal a cake in an airtight container as this may encourage mould growth.

Rich fruit cakes keep well, although they are moist, full of flavour and at their best when first made. The cakes do mature with keeping, but all fruit cakes are best eaten within 3 months. If you are going to keep a fruit cake for several months, pour on the alcohol a little at a time at monthly intervals, turning the cake each time.

Light fruit cakes are stored in the same way as rich fruit cakes, but as they contain less fruit, their keeping qualities are not so good. These cakes are at their best when first made, or within one month of baking.

Once the cakes have been marzipanned and iced they must be stored in cardboard boxes, to keep them dust-free, in a warm, dry atmosphere. Avoid damp and cold conditions as they cause the icing to stain and colourings to run.

Servings:
Working out the number of servings from a round or square cake is extremely simple. It depends if you require just a small finger of cake, or a more substantial slice. Whether the cake is round or square, cut across the cake from edge to edge into about 2.5cm (1in) slices, or thinner if desired. Then cut each slice into 4cm (1½in) pieces, or to the size you require. It is then easy to calculate the number of cake slices you can cut from a given size cake. A square cake is larger than a round cake of the same size, and will yield more slices. On a round cake the slices become smaller at the curved edges, so keep this in mind when calculating the servings.

Rich Fruit Cake Chart

Cake Tin (Pan) Size	13cm (5in) square 15cm (6in) round	15cm (6in) square 17.7cm (7in) round	17.5cm (7in) square 20cm (8in) round
Raisins	125g (4oz/⅔ cup)	185g (6oz/1 cup)	250g (8oz/1½ cups)
Sultanas	125g (4oz/⅔ cup)	185g (6oz/1 cup)	250g (8oz/1½ cups)
Currants	125g (4oz/⅔ cup)	125g (4oz/⅔ cup)	155g (5oz/1 cup)
Dried apricots, chopped	60g (2oz/⅓ cup)	90g (3oz/½ cup)	125g (4oz/¾ cup)
Glacé (candied) cherries, quartered	90g 3oz/¾ cup)	90g (3oz/¾ cup)	150g (5oz/¾ cup)
Cut mixed peel	30g (1oz/3tbsp)	45g (1½oz/3½tbsp)	60g (2oz/⅓ cup)
Mixed chopped nuts	30g (1oz/¼ cup)	45g (1½oz/⅓ cup)	60g (2oz/½ cup)
Lemon rind, coarsely grated	5ml (1 teaspoon)	7.5ml (1½ teaspoons)	10ml (2 teaspoons)
Lemon juice	15ml (1 tablespoon)	22.5ml (1½ tablespoons)	30ml 2 tablespoons)
Brandy, whisky, sherry	15ml (1 tablespoon)	30ml (2 tablespoons)	45ml (3 tablespoons)
Plain (all-purpose) flour	185g (6oz/1½ cups)	220g (7oz/1¾ cups)	280g (9oz/2¼ cups)
Ground mixed spice	5ml (1 teaspoon)	10ml (2 teaspoons)	15ml (3 teaspoons)
Ground almonds	30g (1oz/¼ cup)	45g (1½oz/⅓ cup)	60g (2oz/½ cup)
Soft dark brown sugar	125g (4oz/½ cup)	155g (5oz/½ cup + 2 tbsp)	220g (7oz/¾ cup)
Butter or margarine, softened	125g (4oz/½ cup)	155g (5oz/½ cup + 2tbsp)	220g (7oz/¾ cup)
Black treacle (molasses)	7.5ml (½ tablespoon)	15ml (1 tablespoon)	22.5ml (1½ tablespoons)
Medium eggs	2	3	4
Approximate cooking time	2 to 2¼ hours	2¼ to 2½ hours	2½ to 2¾ hours

Cake Tin (pan) Size	20cm (8in) square 22.5cm (9in) round	22.5cm (9in) square 25cm (10in) round	25cm (10in) square 27.5cm (11in) round	27.5cm (11in) square 30cm (12in) round
Raisins	280g (9oz/1⅔ cups)	375g (12oz/2¼ cups)	500g (1lb/3 cups)	560g (1lb 2oz/3¼ cups)
Sultanas	280g (9oz/1⅔ cups)	375g (12oz/2¼ cups)	500g (1lb/3 cups)	560g (1lb 2oz/3¼ cups)
Currants	250g (8oz/1½ cups)	350g (10oz/2 cups)	375g (12oz/2¼ cups)	440g (14oz/2¾ cups)
Dried apricots, Chopped	155g (5oz/1 cup)	185g (6oz/1 cup)	220g (7oz/1¼ cups)	250g (8oz/1⅓ cups)
Glacé (candid), cherries quartered	175g (6oz/¾ cup)	220g (7oz/¾ cup)	225g (8oz/1 cup)	280g (9oz/1 cup)
Cut mixed peel	90g (3oz/½ cup)	125g (4oz/⅓ cup)	185g (6oz/1 cup)	250g (8oz/1¼ cups)
Mixed chopped nuts	90g (3oz/¾ cup)	125g (4oz/1 cup)	185g (6oz/1 cup)	250g (8oz/2 cups)
Lemon rind, coarsely grated	12.5ml (2½ teaspoons)	15ml (3 teaspoons)	15ml (1 tablespoon)	22.5ml (1½ tablespoons)
Lemon juice	37.5ml (2½ tablespoons)	45ml (3 tablespoons)	60ml (4 tablespoons)	75ml (5 tablespoons)
Brandy, whisky, Sherry	60ml (4 tablespoons)	75ml (5 tablespoons)	90ml (6 tablespoons)	105ml (7 tablespoons)
Plain (all-purpose) flour	345g (11oz/2¾ cups)	470g (15oz/3¾ cups)	575g (1lb 3oz/4¾ cups)	685g (1lb 6oz/5¼ cups)
Ground mixed spice	15ml (1 tablespoon)	22.5ml (1½ tablespoons)	30ml (2 tablespoons)	45ml (3 tablespoons)
Ground almonds	75g (2½oz/⅔ cup)	90g (3oz/¾ cup)	100g (3½oz/⅔ cup)	155g (5oz/1¼ cups)
Soft dark brown sugar	280g (9oz/1 cup + 2tbsp)	410g (13oz/1⅔ cups)	530g (1lb 1oz/2 cups +tbsp)	625g (1lb 4oz/2½ cups)
Butter or margarine, softened	280g (9oz/1 cup + 2tbsp)	410g (13oz/1⅔ cups)	530g (1lb 1oz/2 cups + 2tbsp)	625g (1lb 4oz/2½ cups)
Black treacle (Molasses)	30ml (2 tablespoons)	37.5ml (2½ tablespoons)	45ml (3 tablespoons)	60ml (4 tablespoons)
Medium eggs	5	7	8	9
Approximate cooking time	3 to 3¼ hours	3½ to 3¾ hours	3¾ to 4 hours	4¾ to 5 hours

Marzipan

Marzipan

Marzipan is a paste made from ground almonds and sugar. The consistency, texture and colour varies according to how the paste is made, but the end result is used for giving cakes a smooth, flat surface before applying icings or sugarpaste.

For added colour marzipan can be tinted or coloured and used for cut-out or moulded decorations.

Homemade marzipan has a taste of its own and can be easily made in manageable quantities. Take care not to over-knead or handle the marzipan when making it as this encourages the oils from the ground almonds to flow and they will eventually seep through the iced surface of the cake, causing staining.

Commercial marzipan is available as white, yellow and raw sugar marzipan. Use the white marzipan for all cakes as it is the most reliable type to use, especially when cakes are being iced in pastel shades or white. The yellow marzipan has added food colouring but may be used for covering rich fruit cakes; the yellow colour can show through if the icing is thinly applied, or may cause yellow staining. This marzipan does not take colour so well and is not really recommended for modelling work.

Raw sugar marzipan may be used in place of other marzipan if you are health conscious. Being dark, it is difficult to colour and to use for decorations. It is available from most health food shops.

Always use fresh, pliable marzipan to obtain the best results, especially for covering a cake.

Be sure to dry the marzipanned cake before applying the icing. Set marzipan ensures a good cake shape during icing and prevents any moisture seeping through from the cake and staining the surface.

Always store the marzipanned cake on a clean cake board in a warm, dry room.

Marzipan Chart

Cake Size	13cm (5in) square 15.5cm (6in) round	15.5 (6in) square 17.5cm (7in) round	17.5cm (7in) square 20cm (8in) round	20cm (8in) square 22.5cm (9in) round	22.5cm (9in) square 25cm (10in) round	25cm (10in) square 27.5cm (11in) round	27.5cm (11in) square 30cm (12in) round
Apricot Glaze	15ml (1 tablespoon)	22.5ml (1½ tablespoons)	30ml (2 tablespoons)	37.5ml (2½ tablespoons)	45ml (3 tablespoons)	45ml (3 tablespoons)	60ml (4 tablespoons)
Marzipan	375g (12oz)	750g (1½lb)	875g (1¾lb)	1kg (2lb)	1.25kg (2½lb)	1.5kg (3lb)	1.75kg (3½lb)

Boiled Marzipan

This marzipan is soft and pliable but not so easy to work with as the kneaded marzipan. It has a good flavour and is used for covering cakes and for simple modelling.

Put the sugar and water in a medium-sized saucepan over a low heat, stirring occasionally until the sugar has dissolved.

Add the cream of tartar and bring quickly to the boil. Boil continuously until the sugar syrup has reached soft ball stage, or registers 116° (240°F).

Remove the saucepan from the heat, stir in the ground almonds and essence until well blended and the mixture turns opaque.

Place the egg whites in a bowl and whisk lightly, add them to the marzipan, stir, and return to the heat to cook for a further 2 minutes.

Lightly dust a work surface with icing sugar, place the marzipan in the centre, cover with cling film until completely cold.

Knead the marzipan until soft and pliable and free from any cracks. Store in a polythene bag in a cool, dry place until required.

Makes 500g (1lb) marzipan

INGREDIENTS
250g (8oz/1 cup)
caster (superfine) sugar
155ml (5fl oz/²⁄₃ cup) water
pinch cream of tartar
185g (6oz/1½ cups) ground almonds
2ml (¼ teaspoon)
almond essence (extract)
1-2 egg whites
icing (confectioner's) sugar, to dust

Kneaded Marzipan

This marzipan is quick and easy to make. Take care not to over-knead the mixture as this causes the oil from the ground almonds to flow, which may cause staining when the icing is applied. If you require a lighter-coloured marzipan, use just the egg white instead of a whole egg.

Place the ground almonds and sugars into a bowl. Stir until evenly mixed.

Make a well in the centre and add the lemon juice, almond essence and enough egg or egg white to mix to a soft but firm dough.

Lightly sprinkle a surface with sieved icing sugar and knead the marzipan until completely smooth and free from cracks.

Wrap in cling film or store in a polythene bag until ready for use.

Tint with food colouring if required and use for modelling or as a top covering for cakes.

Makes 500g (1lb) marzipan.

INGREDIENTS
250g (8oz/2 cups) ground almonds
125g (4oz/½ cup)
caster (superfine) sugar
125g (4oz/1 cup) icing
(confectioner's) sugar, sieved
5ml (1 teaspoon) lemon juice
few drops almond essence (extract)
1 small egg, or
1 large egg white

Raw Sugar Marzipan

This marzipan is very similar to kneaded marzipan but is made with raw, soft brown sugar. This gives it a rich flavour and makes it brown in colour. It is not easy to colour the marzipan, although it will take dark colourings. Use it for covering cakes.

Place the ground almonds and soft brown sugar into a bowl. Stir until evenly mixed.

Make a well in the centre and add the lemon juice, almond essence and enough egg or egg white to mix to a soft but firm dough.

Lightly sprinkle a surface with sieved icing sugar and knead the marzipan until smooth and completely free from cracks.

Wrap in cling film or store in a polythene bag until ready for use.

Makes 500g (1lb) marzipan

INGREDIENTS
250g (8oz/2 cups) ground almonds
250g (8oz/1 cup) raw soft dark or light brown sugar
5ml (1 teaspoon) lemon juice
few drops almond essence (extract)
1 small egg, or
1 large egg white

Apricot Glaze

It is useful to make a large quantity and keep it in a screw-topped jar when marzipanning a number of cakes.

Place the jam and water in a saucepan. Heat gently until the jam has melted. Boil rapidly for half a minute, then strain through a sieve. Rub through as much of the fruit as possible and discard the skins, as these cause the glaze to ferment.

Pour the glaze back into the clean hot jar, which has been heated in the oven, and seal with the lid. Use as required.

Makes 500g (1lb) glaze.

INGREDIENTS
500g (1lb) apricot jam (jelly)
45ml (3 tablespoons) water

Marzipanning a Cake

A well marzipanned cake is essential if the top icing is to be smooth, even and blemish-free. The method of application is the same for all varieties of marzipan.

Unwrap the cake and remove the lining paper. Place the cake on the cake board and roll the top with a rolling pin to flatten slightly.

Brush the top of the cake with apricot glaze. Sprinkle the work surface with sieved icing sugar.

Using two-thirds of the marzipan, knead it until smooth. Roll out to a 5mm (¼in) thickness to match the shape of the top of the cake.

Make sure the marzipan moves freely on the work surface inverting the cake on the centre of the marzipan shape.

Trim off the excess marzipan to within 1cm (½in) of the cake, then using a small flexible palette knife, push the marzipan until it is level with the side of the cake.

Turn the cake rightsideup and place in the centre of the cake board. Brush the sides of the cake with warm apricot glaze.

Knead the trimmings together, taking care not to include any crumbs from the cake. Measure and cut a piece of string the length of one side of a square cake or the circumference of a round cake. Measure and cut

another piece of string the depth of the side of the cake from the board to the top.

Roll out the marzipan to 5mm (¼in) thickness and cut out one side piece for a round cake and four pieces for a square cake, to match the length and width of the string. Knead the trimmings together and re-roll if necessary.

Carefully fit the marzipan on the side of the cake and smooth the joins with a palette knife. Leave in a warm, dry place for at least 24 hours to dry before icing.

1. Roll the top of the fruit cake to flatten the fruit.

2. Brush the top with warm apricot glaze.

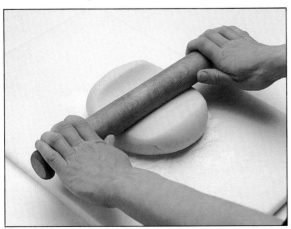

3. Roll out the marzipan on a lightly sugared surface.

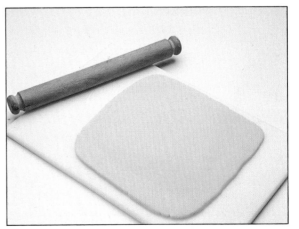

4. Marzipan rolled out to 5mm (¼in) thickness.

5. Fruit cake inverted on to centre of marzipan. Trim the marzipan to within 1cm (½in) of the cake.

6. Use a small palette knife and press the excess marzipan into the side, making it level with the edge of the cake.

7. Inverted cake on the cake board, with a flat square top.

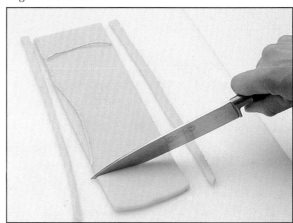

8. Use two pieces of string to measure the width and length of the side of the cake and cut the marzipan strip to size.

9. Fit the marzipan strip on to the side of apricot glazed cake.

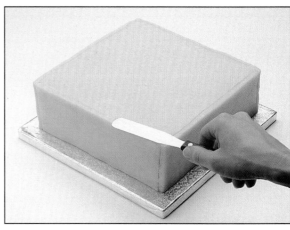

10. Use a small palette knife to smooth all the joins together.

Marzipanning a Cake for Sugarpaste

1. Brush the top and sides of the cake with warmed apricot glaze. Sprinkle the work surface lightly with sieved icing (confectioner's) sugar.

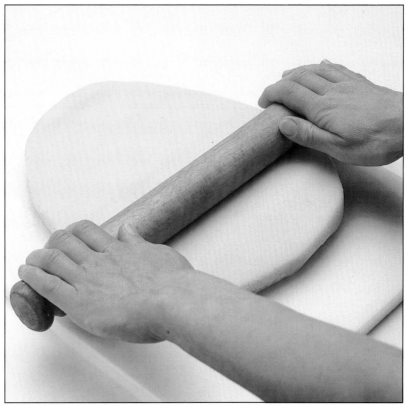

2. Knead the marzipan into a smooth ball. Roll out in the shape of the cake to a 5mm (¼in) thickness, and large enough to cover the whole cake.

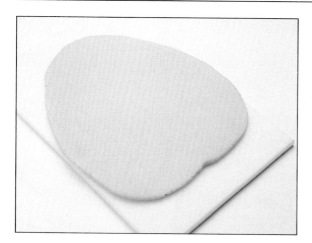

3. Make sure the marzipan moves freely, then roll the marzipan loosely around the rolling pin.

4. Place the supported marzipan over the cake and carefully unroll so that the marzipan falls evenly over the cake.

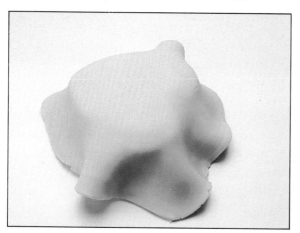

5. Smooth the marzipan over the top and down the sides, allowing the marzipan to fit at the base of the cake without stretching.

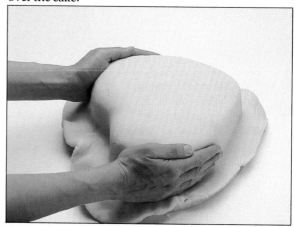

6. Using clean, dry hands, gently rub the top of the cake in circular movements to make a smooth, glossy finish to the marzipan.

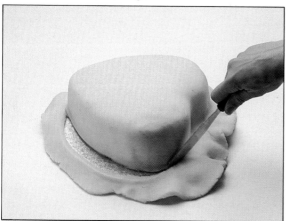

7. Using a sharp knife, trim the excess marzipan from the base of the cake, cutting down on to the board.

8. Leave in a warm, dry place for at least 24 hours before icing.

Decorating Ideas

Marzipan is smooth, soft, easy to work and an ideal base for royal icing and sugarpaste. It can be coloured in various shades with food colourings, cut into shapes moulded into flowers, animals and figures.

Cutouts

This is a simple way of decorating a cake with coloured marzipan cut into a variety of shapes. Tint several pieces of marzipan with food colourings to the required colours, see below. Roll out evenly on a sugared surface until about 3mm (⅛in) thick. Using small aspic, cocktail or biscuit cutters, cut out a variety of shapes. Arrange the cutout shapes in an attractive design on the cake and secure with apricot glaze.

Small flower and leaf cutters may be used to make a flower design; an arrangement of stems and other leaves can be cut out from thin strips of coloured marzipan.

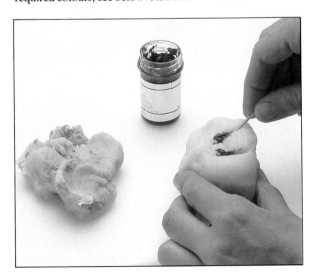

Used as a cake covering on its own, it combines colour, texture and flavour without the sweetness of icing (confectioner's) sugar. Once the cake has been covered in marzipan it can be decorated very simply by crimping the edges, applying cutouts, inlays and marzipan marquetry.

Crimper Designs

These quick, easy and effective designs are created with crimping tools which are available from most kitchen shops or cake decorating suppliers. They come in different shapes: straight, curve, scallops, ovals, 'V', hearts, diamonds, zig-zag.

To obtain an even crimped design, it is helpful to place an elastic band over the crimpers to prevent them springing apart and to adjust the size of the opening to give the required pattern. Try out the design on a spare piece of marzipan before decorating the cake.

Frilling Marzipan

Roll out thin strips of marzipan, making sure the strips move freely. Roll a cocktail stick or the end of a fine paintbrush backwards and forwards creating a thin frilled edge. Make several pieces and apply around the base or sides of the cake, securing with the apricot glaze.

Marquetry

Marquetry in marzipan can be used for making colourful and effective cutouts; it looks a very complicated process but when you know how, it really is quite easy.

Use two or more coloured pieces of marzipan and ensure they are all the same size for each strip. Place the pieces together in a line and roll out evenly to about 3mm (⅛in) thickness, making one piece of marzipan with coloured strips; trim to shape. Cut out the shapes required using shaped cutters or make a cardboard template by tracing around a shape. Try cutting out pieces of marzipan from a shape and replace the cutout piece with other coloured pieces of marzipan.

Christmas Cracker

Make a basic Swiss Roll (Jelly Roll) using a 3-egg quantity of mixture baked in a 32.5cm x 22.5cm (13in x 9in) shallow Swiss Roll (Jelly Roll) tin; fill with apricot jam and roll up.

Colour 375g (12oz) marzipan with red food colouring. On a lightly sugared surface, roll out the marzipan thinly and trim to an oblong 30cm x 25cm (12in x 10in). Brush the Swiss Roll with apricot glaze and place across the width of the marzipan oblong. Enclose the swiss roll in the marzipan trim and press the joins together. Roll over so that the join is underneath and place on a cake board. Smooth the surface and squeeze the ends to form a cracker shape. Using a pair of scissors dipped in icing (confectioner's) sugar, snip both ends of the cracker to form a frill, or flute the ends of the cracker with your fingers dipped in cornflour (cornstarch).

Colour 125g (4oz) marzipan with green food colouring. Roll out thinly and cut out six holly leaves using a holly cutter. Mark the veins with a knife and bend each leaf over a piece of dowel; leave to dry. Arrange on top of the cracker with a few berries made from the trimmings of the red marzipan secure with apricot glaze. Trim the frills with thin strips of green marzipan or ribbons. Leave to set.

Lesson 5

Sugarpaste

Commercial Sugarpaste

Although there are many recipes for homemade sugarpaste, there are certainly times when ready-made pastes are better or more convenient to use.

There are several types of sugarpaste on the market, basically the same kind of recipe but packaged under different names. Textures may vary and some are easier to work with than others. It is a good idea to try a small quantity first to see if it is suitable for the job you require, before purchasing a large quantity.

Sugarpaste is available from large supermarkets and cake decorating shops from 250g (8oz) packs up to 5kg (12lb) boxes, it may be tinted any shade and used very successfully for covering cakes, and for modelling into sugar decorations.

Keep the sugarpaste sealed in a polythene bag; knead in a little boiled water if the outside becomes dry and crumbly, or cut off the dried outer edges.

Fondant Icing

This is a cooked fondant icing which needs careful attention when boiling the sugar syrup. The longer it is kneaded, the whiter and silkier it becomes. When used to cover small or large sponge cakes, it produces a smooth satin finish and may be shaped into small decorations.

Put the white fat, lemon juice and water into a medium-sized saucepan. Heat gently, stirring occasionally, until the fat has melted. Stir in 250g (8oz/2 cups) of sugar and keep stirring until the sugar has dissolved. Leave the saucepan over a low heat until the mixture boils. Remove the saucepan from the heat.

Gradually add enough of the remaining sugar to form a soft paste, beating well after each addition.

Lightly dust the work surface with icing (confectioner's) sugar, then knead the icing continually until smooth, silky and no longer sticky, kneading in more sugar if necessary.

Tint with food colouring if desired, then use immediately for covering a cake and for making small decorations.

Makes 875g (1¾lbs) fondant icing.

INGREDIENTS
60g (2oz/4 tablespoons) white vegetable fat (shortening)
30ml (2 tablespoons) lemon juice
30ml (2 tablespoons) water
750g (1½lbs/5¼ cups) icing (confectioner's) sugar, seived

Making Fondant Icing

1. Measure the water and lemon juice and add to the saucepan containing the white fat.

2. Sift 250g (8oz/2 cups) of the measured icing sugar into the saucepan containing the melted white fat, water and lemon juice.

3. Bring the sugar syrup to the boil.

4. Gradually add the remaining sieved icing sugar.

5. Stir well after each addition of icing sugar.

6. Beat the fondant icing until smooth.

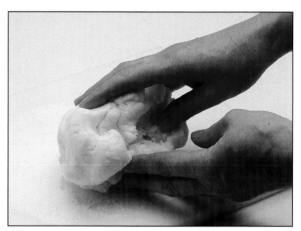

7. Quickly knead the fondant icing on a lightly icing-sugared surface.

Gelatine Icing

An easy-to-make sugarpaste, which handles well being very pliable yet not sticky. Ideal for covering cakes, or tint and use as a modelling paste. It sets hard enough to support a tiered cake, but also cuts easily.

Half-fill a saucepan with water and bring to the boil, then remove from the heat. Place the gelatine and water in a heatproof bowl over the saucepan of hot water. Stir occasionally until the gelatine has dissolved. Add the liquid glucose and glycerine and stir until liquid and warm. Remove the bowl from the saucepan.

Stir the sugar into the gelatine mixture using a wooden spoon. As the mixture begins to bind together, knead into a ball.

Dust work surface lightly with icing (confectioner's) sugar and knead icing until white, smooth and free from cracks. Store in a plastic bag, or wrap in cling film.

Makes 875g (1¾lb) gelatine paste.

INGREDIENTS
15g (½oz/2 envelopes) powdered gelatine
45ml (3 tablespoons) water
45ml (3 tablespoons) liquid glucose
15ml (1 tablespoon) glycerine
few drops of vanilla or almond essence (extract), optional
750g (1½lb/5¼ cups) icing (confectioner's) sugar, sieved

Quick Sugarpaste

This is a quick and easy icing to make. Once it is made, it can be tinted and used to ice all types of cakes. It is soft and pliable enough for moulding all types of sugar decorations. It dries firmly, but not hard enough to support another cake.

Place the egg white and liquid glucose in a clean bowl. Add the sugar and mix together with a wooden spoon. Knead together with the fingers until the mixture forms a ball. Dust work surface lightly with icing sugar and knead until smooth and free from cracks.

Wrap the icing completely in cling film or store in a polythene bag with all the air excluded.

Use white, or tint with food colourings for covering cakes and moulding decorations. On drying it sets firm, but not hard and brittle. If the icing is too soft and sticky to handle, knead in some more sieved sugar until it becomes firm and pliable. If the sugarpaste dries out and becomes hard, knead in a little boiled water until soft and pliable, or cut off the dried outer edges.

Makes 625g (1¼lb) icing.

INGREDIENTS
1 egg white
30ml (2 tablespoons) liquid glucose
500g (1lb/4 cups) icing
(confectioner's) sugar, sieved

Making Quick Sugarpaste

1. Measure the liquid glucose and add it to the bowl containing the egg white.

2. Sift the icing sugar into the bowl.

3. Stir the icing sugar, egg white and liquid glucose together.

4. The mixture beginning to bind together.

5. Use your fingers to form the mixture into a ball.

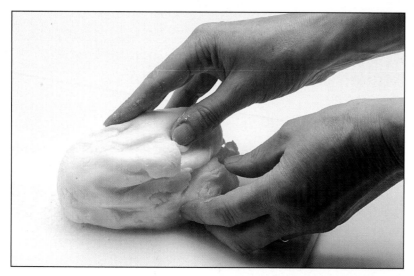

6. Knead on a lightly icing-sugared surface.

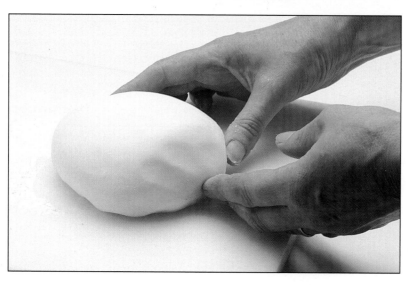

7. Sugarpaste kneaded until smooth and silky.

Covering a Cake with Sugarpaste

1. Brush the cake with sherry or cooled, boiled water to moisten the surface of the marzipan so that the sugarpaste will stick.

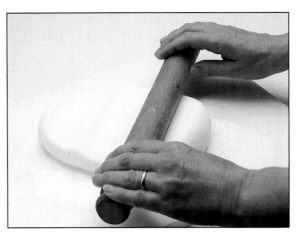

2. Roll out the sugarpaste on a lightly icing-sugared surface.

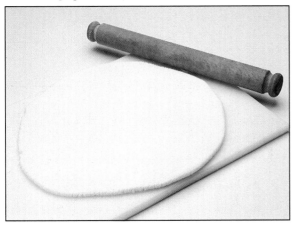

3. Sugarpaste rolled out 7.5cm (3in) larger than the top of the cake.

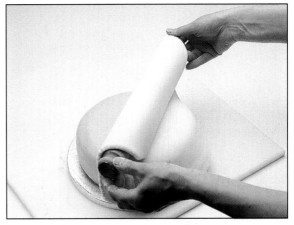

4. Support the sugarpaste with the rolling pin and unroll, over the top of the marzipanned cake.

Covering a Cake with Quick Sugarpaste or Gelatine Icing

Place the marzipanned cake on a turntable and brush the surface with a little sherry or spirit such as kirsch or gin, or with cooled, boiled water.

Sprinkle the work surface with sieved icing (confectioner's) sugar to prevent the icing sticking. Roll out the icing, using more sugar if necessary, to a round or square 7.5cm (3in) larger than the top of the cake.

Lift the icing carefully over the top of the cake, supported by a rolling pin, brushing off any excess sugar. Using well-cornfloured (cornstarched) hands smooth the icing over the top and then down the side of the cake so that the excess icing is at the base, removing any air bubbles between the surfaces.

Trim the excess icing off with a knife and, still with hands dusted, rub the surface in circular movements to make the icing smooth and glossy.

Knead the trimmings together and seal in cling film or a polythene bag to use for decorations.

5. The cake completely covered by the sugarpaste.

6. Gently press the sugarpaste onto the cake, starting at the top and carefully smoothing around the sides so that the excess sugarpaste is at the base of the cake on the board.

7. Use a knife to trim away the excess sugarpaste from the base of the cake.

8. The cake smoothly covered with sugarpaste, ready to decorate.

Making a Painted Sugarpaste Plaque

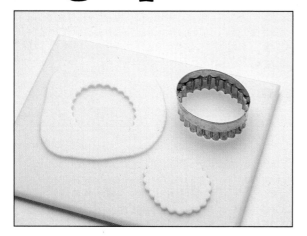

1. Use an oval or circular-shaped cutter to cut out the plaque from thinly rolled out sugarpaste.

2. Use a pen food colouring to draw the outline of the design onto the dry sugar plaque.

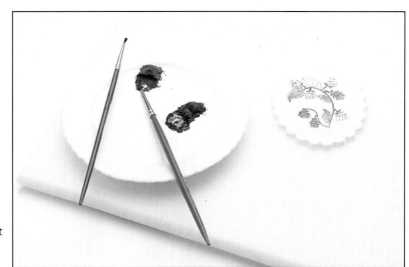

3. Paint the design using fine paint brushes and powdered food colourings with water.

4. The completed painted design.

5. A selection of painted sugar plaques.

Sugarpaste Quantities

Cake Sizes	13cm (5in) square 15.5cm (6in) round	15.5cm (6in) square 17.5cm (7in) round	17.5cm (7in) square 20cm (8in) round	20cm (8in) square 22.5cm (9in) round	22.5cm (9in) square 25cm (10in) round	25cm (10in) square 27.5cm (11in) round	27.5cm (11in) square 30cm (12in) round
Quick Sugarpaste or Gelatine Icing	500g (1lb)	750g (1½lb)	875g (1¾lb)	1kg (2lb)	1.25kg (2½lb)	1.5kg (3lb)	1.75kg (3½lb)

Decorating Ideas

A cake covered in sugarpaste looks so delicate and pretty that it hardly needs decorating; the soft lines and silky finish requires a dainty finishing touch.

Marbling

Sugarpaste lends itself to tinting in all shades, and a very effective way of colouring is to only partially knead the food colouring into the sugarpaste, giving a marbled effect to the icing. Another method is to use two even-sized pieces of sugarpaste, each coloured a different shade. Roll each colour into four thin rolls and place them together, alternating the colours, forming a stack. Roll out thinly to give a marbled effect and use to cover a cake, or for cutout work.

Crimping

Use the same method as marzipan crimping. Ensure the crimper is clean and dusted with cornflour (cornstarch). Only crimp on a freshly sugarpasted cake or the icing will be too rigid and may crack. Try out the design on a spare piece of sugarpaste before attempting to decorate the cake. Remember to release the crimper fully each time it is used to mark the pattern or the icing may tear.

Painted Designs

Try out this skill on a sugarpaste plaque or a runout sugar piece. If a mistake occurs, it gives you the chance to make another painted design. This form of decorating may be applied on to the surface of a royal iced or sugarpasted cake when you are confident enough to paint directly onto the surface.

Almost any design or shape can be transferred to the plaque or cake surface, either drawn freehand or traced. For festive designs, draw Christmas trees, bells, candles, holly leaves and lanterns. Other shapes could include flowers, animals, figures and simple scenes.

Use food colouring pens, available in assorted colours which are ideal for outlines and small work. Liquid, paste or powdered food colourings may be used and applied with a fine brush.

Ensure the surface on to which you are applying the design is completely dry. If you are making a sugar plaque, roll out the sugarpaste thinly and cut

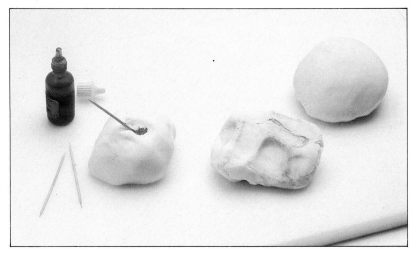

1. Add food colouring to the sugarpaste using a cocktail stick. The colour can be partially kneaded in for a marbled look, or completely kneaded in for an even colour.

2. Coloured sugarpaste rolled out thinly and cut into different shapes using a variety of cocktail, alphabet and numeral cutters.

out an oval, round or square shape. Leave it until completely dry, then trace or draw a freehand design on to the surface. Using the food colouring pens or food colourings and a paintbrush, paint in the details. If you are using food colourings, choose a very fine paintbrush and place small drops of colouring onto separate pieces of greaseproof paper. Dip the brush into the chosen colour and blot the end with kitchen paper, eliminating any drops of colouring. Carefully paint the design, cleaning the brush

thoroughly between colours.

Make a border design on the cake by painting dots, lines or curves to create an attractive pattern. Always practise on a spare piece of sugarpaste before attempting the main design.

Cutouts make an instant decoration for a sugarpaste cake; simply colour the icing in the chosen colours, roll out thinly and cut out small icing shapes using aspic or cocktail cutters. Press these shapes on to the sides and top of the cake, securing with egg white if necessary.

Royal Icing

Royal Icing

To produce a beautifully royal iced cake it is essential to make good royal icing, otherwise it is impossible to obtain a smooth coating. Everything must be spotless when making the icing as little bits that get into the icing will come to the surface on a flat coat.

Fresh egg whites or dried albumen may be used, both producing good results. A little lemon juice helps to strengthen the albumen in fresh egg whites, but care must be taken not to add too much as this will make the icing short, causing it to break during piping and it will be difficult to spread. Do not add glycerine to egg albumen as it does not set as hard as fresh egg white icing.

Adding the icing (confectioner's) sugar must be a gradual process, with plenty of mixing rather than beating during each addition of sugar, until the required consistency is reached.

Royal icing should be light and slightly glossy in texture, and should be capable of forming a peak with a fine point when a wooden spoon is drawn slowly out of the icing. This ensures that the icing will flow easily for piping or spread smoothly for coating, even though the consistencies may be different.

Royal icing made with too much sugar added too quickly will form a dull, heavy icing and be grainy in appearance. It will be difficult to work

with, producing bad results. As it sets it will be chalky in appearance instead of having a sparkle. It will soon become short and break when piped.

The icing must be covered to exclude all air and prevent the surface from setting. Damp cling film is a good way to seal the surface, or use an airtight container filled to the top with icing to exclude any air.

Use small quantities of icing at a time in a separate bowl from the main batch, covering with damp muslin (cheesecloth) during use. Keep the icing well scraped down; if this icing does become dry, causing hard bits, the whole batch of royal icing will not be affected.

Covering with a damp cloth is fine during short periods but if left overnight the icing will absorb all the moisture from the cloth, causing the consistency to be diluted.

If the icing is too stiff, add egg white or reconstituted egg albumen to make it softer. If the icing is too soft, gradually stir in more icing (confectioner's) sugar until the icing is of the required consistency.

Consistency

The consistency of royal icing varies for different uses. Stiff for piping, slightly softer for flat or peaked icing, and thinner for runouts.

Piping consistency: when a wooden spoon is drawn out of the icing it should form a fine, sharp point; termed stiff peak.

Flat or Peaked consistency: when the spoon is drawn out of the icing it should form a fine point which curves over at the end; termed soft peak.

Runouts consistency: soft peak to pipe the outlines, and thick cream consistency to fill in the shapes.

Glycerine

Glycerine may be added to royal icing provided that it is not made with egg albumen. Glycerine stops the icing from drying very hard so also makes cutting easier. Do not add glycerine to icing which is to be used for fine tube work, piped flowers or runouts.

Mix the glycerine to the finished icing and beat in. Add 8-10ml (1½-2 teaspoons) to each 500g (1lb/3½ cups) icing (confectioner's) sugar.

Royal Icing 1

This is a traditional icing used to cover celebration cakes. According to the consistency made, it may be used for flat icing, peaked icing or piping designs.

Place the egg whites and lemon juice into a clean bowl. Using a clean wooden spoon, stir to break up the egg whites. Add sufficient icing sugar and mix well to form the consistency of unwhipped cream. Continue mixing and adding small quantities of sugar every few minutes until the desired consistency has been reached, mixing well after each addition.

The icing should be smooth, glossy and light. Stir in the glycerine. Do not add too much sugar too quickly as this will produce a dull, heavy icing which is difficult to handle.

Allow the icing to rest before using it; cover the surface with a piece of damp cling film and seal well. Stir the icing thoroughly before use to disperse the air bubbles, then adjust the consistency if necessary.

This icing is suitable for flat or peaked icing, piping and runouts.

Makes 500g (1lb/3½ cups) royal icing.

INGREDIENTS
2 egg whites
1ml (¼ teaspoon) lemon juice
500g (1lb/3½ cups) icing (confectioner's) sugar, sieved
5ml (1 teaspoon) glycerine

Making Royal Icing

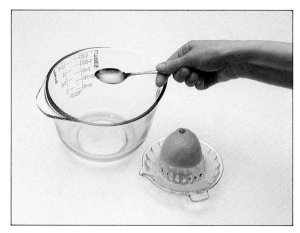

1. Measure the lemon juice and add it to the bowl containing the egg whites.

2. Sift some of the measured icing sugar into the bowl.

3. Using a wooden spoon, stir the icing sugar into the egg whites and lemon juice.

4. Stir in sufficient icing sugar until the consistency is of thick cream, then beat well.

5. Royal icing beaten until smooth and white, after gradually adding enough icing sugar until thick.

6. Soft peak consistency of royal icing, ready to use for flat or peaked icing.

7. Sharp peak consistency of royal icing, ready for piping.

Colouring Royal Icing

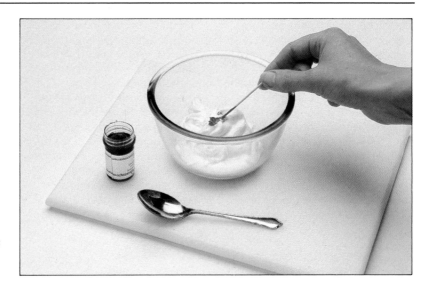

1. Add the food colouring to the royal icing a little at a time using a cocktail stick.

2. Stir the colouring into the icing until blended.

3. Evenly coloured royal icing, ready to use.

Royal Icing 2

Dried powered egg albumen may be used in place of fresh egg whites for royal icing. Simply blend the egg albumen with water and use like egg whites. Used as flat icing for tiered cakes, it sets hard enough to support the weight of the cakes.

Put the egg albumen into a clean bowl, gradually stir in the water and blend well together until the liquid is smooth and free from lumps.

Add sufficient sugar and mix well to the consistency of unwhipped cream. Continue mixing and adding small quantities of sugar every few minutes until the desired consistency has been reached, mixing well after each addition of sugar. The icing may be made in an electric mixer on a slow speed and using a whisk, not a beater.

The finished icing should be smooth, glossy and light. Do not add too much sugar too quickly as this will produce a dull, heavy icing which is difficult to handle.

Allow the icing to settle before using it; cover the surface with a piece of damp cling film and seal well. Stir the icing thoroughly before use to disperse the air bubbles, then adjust the consistency if necessary.

This icing is suitable for flat or peaked icing, piping and runouts. Use double-strength dried egg albumen for runouts so that they will set hard enought to remove from the paper.

Makes 500g (1lb/3½ cups) royal icing.

INGREDIENTS
15ml (1 tablespoon)
dried egg albumen
75ml (5 tablespoons) tepid water
500g (1lb/3½ cups) icing
(confectioner's) sugar, sieved

Flat Icing

Royal icing cannot be applied quickly. Thin layers of icing are applied to the cake in sections and time has to be allowed in between for each to dry.

Make a quantity of royal icing to soft peak consistency and cover with a clean, damp muslin (cheesecloth) to prevent drying make sure the marzipan on the cake is dry and firm, then place the board and cake on a turntable.

Spread a layer of icing about 5mm (¼in) thick evenly over the top of the cake, remove the excess icing from the edges with a small palette knife. Remove from the turntable and place on a rigid surface.

Stand directly in front of the cake with a rule or straight edge poised at the far edge of the cake. Hold the rule or straight edge comfortably in both hands and pull it towards you in one steady movement to smooth the top of the cake.

If the surface is not satisfactory, spread another thin layer of icing over the cake and repeat as above until the icing is smooth.

Remove the excess icing on the side of the cake to neaten the top edge using a small palette knife. Leave to dry for at least 4 hours, or overnight, in a warm, dry place.

Place the cake on a turntable again, spread a layer of icing 5mm (¼in) thick around the side of a round cake. Carefully remove any excess icing from the top edge.

Place a side scraper on to the side of the cake, resting on the board. Pull the side scraper with one hand while rotating the turntable with the other hand, in one continuous steady movement. The side of the cake should be completely smooth. Repeat if necessary.

Carefully pull off the scraper, which will leave a fine pull off mark on the round cake. Using a palette knife, remove the excess icing around the top of the cake. For a square cake, ice two opposite sides. Spread the icing onto one side, pull the side scraper across to smooth. Trim off excess icing and repeat on opposite sides, allowing time in between to dry.

1. Place the marzipanned cake with cake board on the turntable. The royal icing should be at soft peak consistency.

2. Use a small palette knife to spread the icing smoothly over the top of the cake to cover evenly.

3. Remove the excess icing from the top edges of the cake.

4. Steadily pull the straight edge across the top of the cake in one movement to smooth the icing.

5. Trim away the excess icing from the top edges of the cake to neaten before drying.

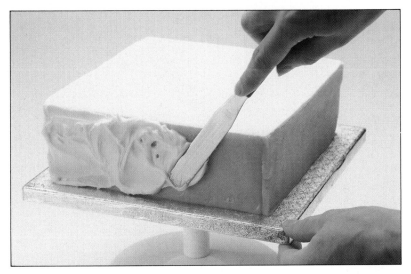

6. Use a small palette knife to smoothly spread the side of the dry cake with icing.

7. Remove the excess icing from the dry icing on the top edge of the cake.

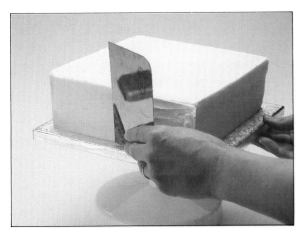

8. Pull the side scraper across the side of the cake. Trim away the excess icing from the top edge and corners of the cake to neaten before drying.

9. The cake covered with one coat of royal icing. Dry before coating again.

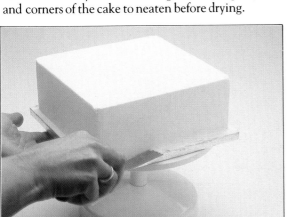

10. Spread a thin layer of icing along one side of the cake board to cover evenly.

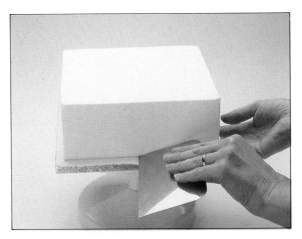

11. Pull the side scraper over the icing on the cake board to smooth.

Royal Icing Quantity Guide

It is difficult to estimate how much royal icing will be used to ice a cake as the quantity varies according to how the icing is applied and to the thickness of layers. The design also has to be taken into account, whether it is just piping, or runouts and sugar pieces.

The best guide to follow when icing cakes is to make up the royal icing in small batches using 1kg (2lb/7 cups) of icing (confectioner's) sugar, which is double the quantity of the recipe. Each batch of icing made is fresh and free from any impurities which may occur when large quantities are made for one cake.

The chart below is a guide for covering each cake with two or three thin layers of flat royal icing.

Cake Size	Quantity of Royal Icing
13cm (5 inch) square.	500g (1lb/3½ cups)
15.5cm (6in) round.	750g (1½lb/4¾ cups)
15cm (6in) square.	
17.5cm (7in) round.	1kg (2lb/7 cups)
17.5cm (7in) square.	
20cm (8in) round.	1.25kg (2½lb/8¾ cups)
20cm (8in) square.	
22.5cm (9in) round.	1.5kg (3lb/10½ cups)
22.5cm (9in) square.	1.75g (3½lb/12¼ cups)
25cm (10in) round.	
25cm (10in) square.	
27.5cm (11in) round.	

Decorating

R oyal icing must be the most versatile icing; it can be smoothed on to a cake to make a perfectly flat base for decorating, or peaked and swirled to give texture to a Christmas cake. It can be piped as curves or lines from different-shaped tubes.

Peaks and Swirls

A simple way to decorate a Christmas cake is with swirls or peaks of icing with a festive centrepiece on the top. To swirl royal icing, quickly spread the top and sides of the cake as evenly as possible. Using a small palette knife, go over the surface again in circular movements to swirl the icing.

To make beautifully even peaks, the icing must be of soft peak consistency. Cover the cake evenly with icing and smooth the top and sides with a palette knife. Using a small, clean palette knife, dip one side into the icing. Starting from the top edge and working around the edge of the cake, press the palette knife onto the icing and pull sharply away to form a peak. Repeat to form about six peaks, then re-dip the palette knife into the icing and repeat to make peaks around the top edge.

Make the second row of peaks, in between the first row, about 10mm (½in) below and continue until the

side is complete. Repeat to peak the top, leaving a smooth area for decorations if necessary. If the top is to be flat, follow the step-by-step guide for flat icing the top of a cake then, when completely dry, peak the sides as above.

Purchased Decorations

Flat or smooth icing takes more time and patience, but by following the step-by-step instructions and with practice, a good standard can be achieved. Once iced smoothly, the cake may be decorated with purchased decorations to suit any occasion. Tie ribbon around the side of the cake and use sugar flowers, or coloured dragées to decorate the top. Cake decorating suppliers have a vast selection to choose from.

Painted Designs

Painting or pen designs may be applied in the same way as the sugarpaste painted designs. Damp is

the main problem as the icing absorbs moisture, causing colours to bleed. Small runout icing plaques can be made in any shape, then the design painted on with either food colourings and a fine paintbrush, or food colouring pens. Store in a warm, dry place.

Coloured Swirls

Coloured icing spread into swirls over the surface is a simple way of introducing colours on to a white royal iced cake. Spread the top and sides of a marzipanned cake with white royal icing. Smooth the top and sides with a palette knife. Tint a small quantity of royal icing; use a small palette knife, dip into the tinted icing and press on to the cake and swirl. Repeat by swirling the icing, evenly spaced, over the top and sides of the cake. Try several shades of icing or contrasting colours to give a variety of swirls on the cake.

Lesson 7

Quick Icings and Frostings

Buttercream

A versatile filling, icing or frosting for almost any type of cake, which can be spread evenly and patterned with a knife or scraper, or piped into designs using different icing tubes. Flavour with chocolate, coffee, orange or lemon rinds.

Place the butter in a bowl and beat until pale and fluffy. Add the icing (confectioner's) sugar a little at a time, beating well after each addition. Beat in the lemon juice, vanilla essence (extract) and any other flavouring if required.

Alternatively, place all the ingredients into a food processor and blend for 30 seconds.

Makes 250g (8oz/1¾ cups)

INGREDIENTS
125g (4oz/½ cup) butter, softened
250g (8oz/1¾ cups) icing
(confectioner's) sugar, sieved
10ml (2 teaspoons) lemon juice
few drops vanilla essence (extract)

VARIATIONS
15ml (1 tablespoon)
cocoa blended with 15ml
(1 tablespoon) of boiling water.
10ml (2 teaspoons) instant coffee
blended with 5ml (1 teaspoon) of
boiling water.
10ml (2 teaspoons) lemon, orange
or lime rind.

Making Buttercream

1. Beat the butter with a wooden spoon until light and fluffy.

2. Sift some of the sugar into the bowl.

3. Stir the sugar into the butter, then beat well after each addition.

4. Add the lemon juice or other flavourings and beat until smooth.

5. Use a cocktail stick to add food colouring to the buttercream.

6. Beat the food colouring into the buttercream.

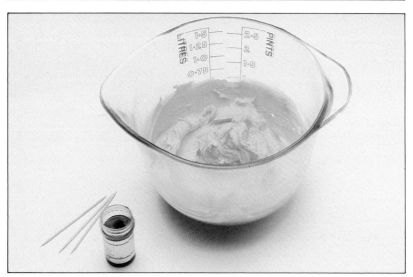

7. Buttercream evenly coloured and ready to use.

8. Spread the buttercream on to the top of the cake using a small palette knife.

9. Cake evenly coated with buttercream before it is smoothed.

10. Smooth the buttercream using a small palette knife dipped into hot water.

American Icing

A pure white icing (frosting) made with white vegetable fat (shortening) instead of butter or margarine. It is light in texture and can be flavoured or coloured if desired. As the icing is white, tinting with food colouring is more accurate.

Place the white fat in a bowl and beat until white and fluffy. Add the icing sugar a little at a time, beating well after each addition. Beat in the vanilla essence and any other flavouring if required.

Alternatively, place all the ingredients into a food processor and blend for 30 seconds.

Makes 250g (8oz/1¾ cup)

INGREDIENTS
125g (4oz/½ cup) white vegetable
fat (shortening)
250g (8oz/1¾ cups) icing
(confectioner's) sugar, sieved
15ml (3 teaspoons) milk
5ml (1 teaspoon) vanilla essence
(extract)

VARIATIONS
15ml (1 tablespoon) cocoa blended
with 15ml (1 tablespoon)
boiling water.
10ml (2 teaspoons) instant coffee
blended with 5ml (1 teaspoon) of
boiling water.
10ml (2 teaspoons) lemon, orange
or lime rind.

Crême au Beurre

A light-textured buttercream suitable for large and small cakes, which keeps the cakes moist. It spreads or pipes well, giving a glossy finish. For best results, make and use it when required; do not chill or freeze until it has been applied to the cake.

Place the sugar and water in a saucepan. Heat gently until the sugar has dissolved, stirring occasionally. Boil rapidly for about 1 minute until the syrup reaches thread stage. Test by placing a little syrup between two teaspoons: when pulled apart, a thread of syrup should form.

Whisk the egg yolks and pour in a steady stream of syrup, whisking all the time. Continue to whisk until the mixture is thick and pale.

Beat the butter in a separate bowl until pale and fluffy; add the egg mixture a little at a time, beating or whisking gently after each addition, until all the egg mixture has been incorporated.

Add any flavourings at this stage, if required, and use at once.

Makes 250g (8oz/1¾ cup)

INGREDIENTS
90g (3oz/6 tablespoons) caster
(superfine) sugar
60ml (4 tablespoons) water
2 egg yolks, beaten
155g (5oz/½ cup + 2tbsp) unsalted
(sweet) butter, softened

Glacé Icing

Suitable for quickly decorating small cakes, Swiss (jelly) rolls or tops of cakes.

Place the sugar into a bowl; using a wooden spoon, gradually stir in the water until the icing is the same consistency as thick cream. Tint with food colouring if desired.

INGREDIENTS
250g (8oz/1¾ cups) icing (confectioner's) sugar, sieved 30-45ml (2-3 tablespoons) boiling water

VARIATIONS
Add 10ml (2 teaspoons) cocoa to the sugar. Replace the water with any fruit juice, or strong black coffee.

Making Crème au Beurre

1. Measure the water and sugar into the saucepan.

2. Dissolve sugar in the water to form sugar solution before boiling to a syrup.

3. Test a little of the boiled sugar syrup between two teaspoons: a thread is formed when the spoons are pulled apart.

4. Pour a thin stream of sugar syrup into the beaten egg yolks.

5. Whisk well after each addition. Whisk the mixture until light and thick.

6. Beat the butter with a wooden spoon until light and fluffy.

7. Pour the egg mixture into the butter.

8. Whisk the mixture gently after each addition until light and creamy.

9. Add some grated orange rind to flavour the Crème au Beurre.

10. Use a spatula to carefully mix in the orange rind without beating.

Quick Frosting

A quickly-made icing (frosting) suitable for pouring over cakes to give a smooth, satin finish or for spreading with a knife to give a textured appearance.

Half-fill a saucepan with water and bring to the boil, then remove from the heat. Place the butter, milk and icing sugar in a heatproof bowl over a saucepan of hot water. Stir this occasionally until melted, then beat with a wooden spoon until smooth.

Use immediately to pour over a cake to coat evenly, or leave until thicker, then spread over a cake to give a textured finish.

This quantity will cover a 17.5-20cm (7-8in) square cake, or a 20-22.5cm (8-9in) round cake.

INGREDIENTS
60g (2oz/4 tablespoons) butter
45ml (3 tablespoons) milk
250g (8oz/1¾ cups) icing (confectioner's) sugar, sieved

VARIATION 1
Fruit or Coffee Frosting: replace the milk with any flavour fruit juice, or strong black coffee.

VARIATION 2
Fudge Frosting: replace 90g (3oz/¾ cup) of icing (confectioner's) sugar with dark, soft brown sugar.

VARIATION 3
Chocolate Frosting: add 15ml (1 tablespoon) of cocoa to the icing (confectioner's) sugar or 60g (2oz) of plain (semi-sweet or unsweetened) chocolate to the milk and butter.

Chocolate Fudge Icing

A rich chocolate icing (frosting) suitable for coating, filling and piping onto cakes. Use the icing immediately to give a smooth, glossy finish or leave it to thicken, then spread with a small palette knife to give a swirly textured finish.

Half-fill a saucepan with water and bring to the boil, then remove from the heat. Place the chocolate and butter in a heat-proof bowl over the saucepan of hot water. Stir this occasionally until melted.

Add the egg and stir with a wooden spoon until mixed together and well blended. Remove the bowl from the saucepan, stir in the sugar and beat until smooth.

Use immediately for pouring over a cake smoothly or leave to cool for a thicker consistency.

This quantity will cover a 17.5-20cm (7-8in) square cake, or a 20-22.5cm (8-9in) round cake.

INGREDIENTS
125g (4oz/4 squares) plain (semi-sweet or unsweetened) chocolate
60g (2oz/4 tablespoons) butter
1 egg, beaten
185g (6oz/1¼ cups) icing (confectioner's) sugar, seived

Simple Decorations

Buttercream is easy to use for decorating a cake. It can be coloured and flavoured, used as a cake covering, topping, filling and for piping. The consistency remains the same for all finishes.

Iced Top and Coated Sides

Sandwich a sponge cake together with buttercream and spread the sides to coat evenly. Press chopped nuts, coconut, chocolate strands (vermicelli) or crushed macaroons on to the side of the cake to coat evenly. Spread the top as evenly and smoothly as possible. Make a pretty edging with red and green coloured cherries cut into thin slices and arranged around the edge, or arrange with a selection of marzipan fruits or sugar flowers.

Scraper Design

A side scraper can produce a very attractive pattern when used to smooth the icing on the sides and top of a cake, or in a zig-zag movement on the top. It looks like a plastic side scraper but the edge is serrated, rather than flat.

Spread the top and sides of the cake with Crême au Beurre, buttercream, chocolate or American icing (frosting). Place the side scraper on to the side of the cake and pull across or around the side in one movement to make the pattern. Repeat to pattern the top if desired and decorate with fruit rinds cut into tiny shapes using aspic cutters, chocolate dots, nuts cherries, angelica or sugar flowers.

Finishes with Simple Icings

Lines: Buttercream lends itself to various finishes, being soft and easy to spread. Try using a small palette knife to create an attractive finishes. Spread the top and sides of a cake with buttercream, Crême au Beurre, chocolate or American icing (frosting). Using a small palette knife on the top of the cake, spread the icing backwards and forwards in a continuous movement to make a lined pattern. To create the same pattern on the sides, place the palette knife at the base of the cake and work up and down, pressing the knife into the icing (frosting) marking the same pattern. Apply a few nuts or sugar flowers to make a pretty border.

Peaks: These can also be formed in soft icing (frosting) just like royal icing peaks. Once the top and sides of a cake have been spread evenly with icing (frosting), press a small palette knife onto the icing and pull sharply away to form a peak. Ensure the icing (frosting) is not too firm or the palette knife may pull the sponge cake away with it, causing crumbs. Peak the side, working around the top of the cake and gradually down to the base, keeping the top smooth. Arrange some mimosa balls and angelica, or split almonds and crystallied violets to make a flower design.

Edible Decorations: Many ingredients can make attractive decorations. Place some cocoa or coffee on a piece of kitchen paper, then dip a skewer into the powder and press onto an iced cake to make a line. Repeat, marking lines in both directions to form a lattice design. Very fine lines of chopped nuts may be used in the same way. Melted chocolate drizzled on to the surface makes a cake look special.

Coloured Swirls: The use of coloured icing spread into swirls over the surface is a simple way of introducing colours onto a cake iced (frosted) with buttercream. Spread the top and sides of a cake with buttercream; smooth with a palette knife. Tint a small quantity of buttercream. Use a small palette knife, dip into the tinted icing (frosting) and press on to the cake and swirl. Repeat by swirling the icing (frosting), evenly spaced, over the top and sides of the cake. Try several shades of one colour icing or contrasting colours to give a variety of swirls on the cake.

Quick Icing and Frosting quantities for Buttercream, Crême au Beurre and American Icing

Cake Size	17.5cm (7in) square 17.5-20cm (7in-8in) round	20cm (8in) square 22.5cm (9in) round	22.5cm (9-10in) square 25-27.5cm (10-11in) round
Icing and Frosting Quantity	250g (8oz/1¾ cups)	375g (12oz/2⅔ cups)	500g (1lb/3½ cups)

Introduction to Piping

Basic Piping

The skill of using a piping bag is worth mastering. A purchased plastic or fabric piping bag or homemade paper one, fitted with a plain or fancy piping tube, can produce shells and scrolls, bold edgings or very fine filigree work.

Although piping appears to be complicated, with patience, practise and a few simple guidelines, you will discover how easy it is.

Icing: Before using any piping equipment it is essential to have the icing at the correct consistency. When a wooden spoon is drawn out of royal icing, it should form a fine but sharp point. If the icing is too stiff it will be very difficult to squeeze out of the bag; if too soft the icing will be difficult to control and the piped shapes will lose their definition.

Commercial Bags: Piping bags made of a washable fabric are available from most cake specialist or kitchen shops. They are especially good to use if you are a beginner as they are easy to handle. Sizes vary from small to large and are ideal for piping cream, buttercream and icing onto gâteaux and simple sponge cakes. Plastic bags for piping are also available.

Paper Piping Bags: These can also be purchased ready-made, but that is rather expensive as they are so simple to make. The great advantage of paper piping bags is that they can be made in advance in various sizes and can be used without a piping tube, simply by snipping the end into different shapes. After use they are thrown away, or, if the icing runs out, simple transfer the tube to a new paper bag. Choose good quality greaseproof (waxed) paper for making the bags and follow the instructions below carefully.

Piping Tubes: These are available in a wide variety of shapes and sizes, metal and plastic, with or without a collar, so it is quite daunting to know which ones to choose. For beginners, it is advisable to start with a small selection, choosing perhaps two writing tubes and a small, medium and large star tube. After mastering these, build up a collection for trying

out new piping designs.

Straight-sided metal tubes fit commercial bags as well as paper piping bags and give a clean, sharp result. Kept clean and stored carefully they will never need replacing and are worth the extra expense.

Some piping tubes have a collar with a screw thread at the top. This fits some commercial bags and icing syringes and has to be fitted with a screw piece. Once the bag or syringe is filled with icing, any tube with a collar may be attached so the tubes can be changed while piping. The disadvantage of these bags and tubes is that sometimes the screw is forced out of the end of the bag while piping. A collar tube is unsuitable for use with a paper piping bag.

Making a Paper Piping Bag

1. Fold the rectangle of greaseproof (waxed) paper diagonally in half so that the two triangles are equal.

2. Cut into two triangles.

3. Fold the blunt end of the triangle over into a sharp cone to the centre and hold in position.

4. Fold the sharp end of the triangle over the cone.

5. Hold all the points together at the back of the cone, ensuring the point of the cone is sharp.

6. Turn the points inside the top edge to hold the bag firmly.

Trimming the Paper Piping Bag

1. Cut off the point of the bag, at an angle. Make the second cut across the pointed end of the bag to form an inverted V shape.

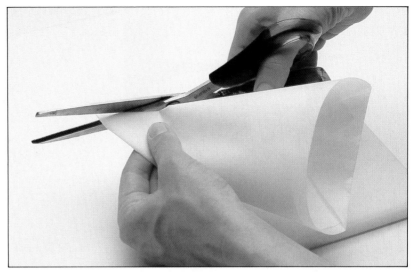

2. The open V shape at the end of the bag, ready to pipe leaves.

3. Cut the W shape at the end of the piping bag, after the point has been cut off.

Fitting a Piping Tube and Filling the Bag

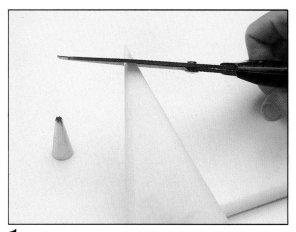

1. Snip the point off the end of the piping bag.

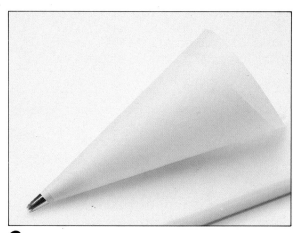

2. The bag fitted with a star tube.

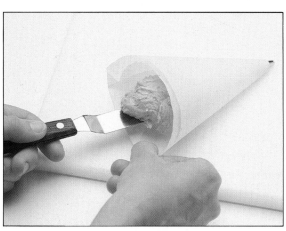

3. Use a small palette knife to place the icing in the piping bag.

4. Press the bag over the icing and withdraw the palette knife.

5. Fold the top corners of the bag into the centre.

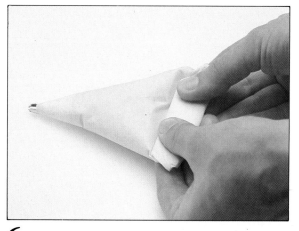

6. Fold down the top of the bag, ready for piping.

Simple Piping

Piping is the obvious choice when decorating a cake, but it is easy to be discouraged by complicated piping designs. Begin with these simple designs and practise until you are proficient, then you may apply these skills to decorating a cake.

Choose just a simple star tube and fit it into a greaseproof paper piping bag to pipe swirls, scrolls and shells. Tint some buttercream or royal icing of sharp peak consistency with a small amount of food colouring. Half-fill the piping bag, fold down the top and squeeze the icing to the end of the tube. Place the icing tube just onto the surface of the cake. Pipe a swirl of icing in a circular movement, stop pressing the bag and pull up sharply to break the thread. Repeat to pipe swirls around the top edge and base of the cake if desired.

To pipe a star shape from the same tube, hold the bag straight above the surface of the cake. Press the icing out to form a star on the edge of the cake, then stop pressing and pull up sharply to break the icing; repeat to make a neat border.

To pipe scrolls hold the piping bag at an angle so that the piping tube is almost on its side.
Pipe some icing on the top edge of the cake to secure the scroll. Pipe outwards in a circular movement and return the piping tube to the edge of

the cake. Stop pressing the bag and break off the icing. Repeat again, but pipe the icing inwards to the cake in a circular movement, then return the piping tube just to the edge. This is piping scrolls curving inwards and outwards. For a different design, pipe the scrolls in one direction only.

To pipe shells, hold the piping bag at an angle to the cake so that the piping tube is almost on its side. Press out some icing and secure to the surface of the cake, press gently move the tube forward, then move it slowly up, over and down almost like a rocking movement. Stop pressing and break off the icing by pulling the tube towards you. Repeat, piping the icing onto the end of the first shell to make a shell edging.

To pipe lines, fit the piping bag with a plain writing tube and fill with icing. Pipe a line of icing, securing the end to the surface of the cake. Continue to pipe the icing just above the surface of the cake, allowing the thread to fall in a straight or curved line. Stop pressing the bag and sharply break off the line of icing.

To pipe leaves, cut the end of the greaseproof paper piping bag into an

inverted V. Fill with icing and press the icing to the end of the bag. Place the end on the surface of the cake. Press out the icing to form a leaf shape, press harder to make a larger leaf then sharply break off the icing. Repeat to make a pretty border, or just to decorate flowers or to make a design.

To pipe a star border, use a greaseproof paper piping bag, trim the end into a W shape and fill with icing. Place the pointed end on the surface of the cake at an angle and pipe out a star shape. Repeat, piping the stars close together to form a border design.

To pipe basketweave, fit a paper piping bag with a ribbon or basketweave tube. Pipe a vertical line from the top of the cake to the bottom. Pipe 2cm (¾in) lines across the vertical line at intervals the width of the tube. Pipe another vertical line of icing on the edge of the horizontal lines, then pipe short lines of icing in between the spaces across the vertical line to form a basketweave. Repeat until the cake is completely covered.

Simple Piping

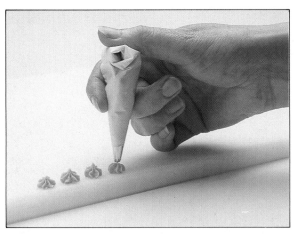

1. Hold the piping bag vertically and pipe a simple star of icing. Stop pressing the bag to stop the flow of icing and lift up sharply.

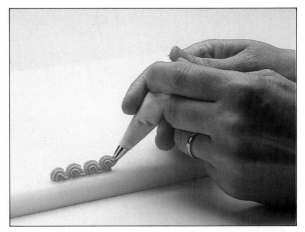

2. Hold the bag at an angle and pipe a row of shells. Stop pressing the bag to finish each shell, before piping the next one.

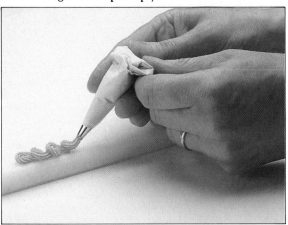

3. Hold the piping bag at an angle and pipe reverse scrolls as a border. Pipe one scroll towards the edge and the second scroll away from the edge.

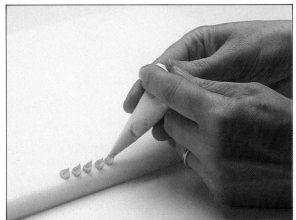

4. Use a greaseproof paper piping bag snipped into a V shape and pipe leaf shapes as a border.

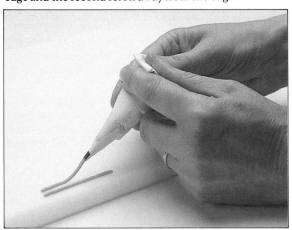

5. Use a plain writing tube to pipe lines of icing. Secure the end of the icing to the surface, then pipe allowing the thread to fall in position.

6. Pipe lines of icing; break off the thread by sharply lifting the tube upwards.

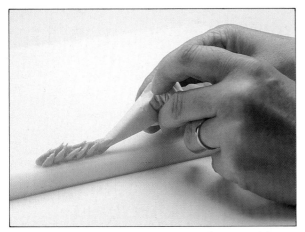

7. Using a greaseproof paper piping bag snipped into a W shape and piping a border design.

8. To pipe a basketweave, pipe a vertical line of icing, then overpipe horizontal lengths of icing at evenly spaced intervals.

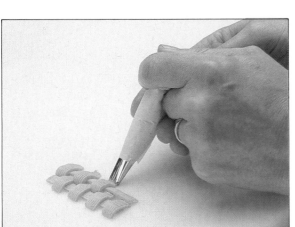

9. Pipe second vertical line of icing over the short horizontal lines, then repeat the pattern.

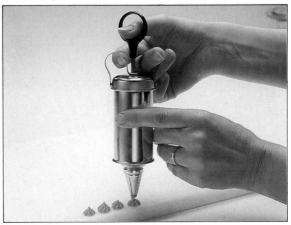

10. An icing syringe fitted with a star tube in the vertical position to pipe stars of icing.

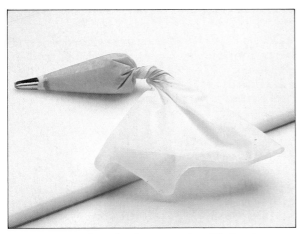

11. A purchased nylon piping bag filled with icing, fitted with a star tube.

12. Hold the nylon piping bag in an upright position and squeeze the top to pipe stars.

Simple Decorations

Once you have mastered the skills of piping, it is the most effective form of decoration on a cake. Piping can quickly transform a plain, everyday cake into something quite spectacular.

Buttercream Sponge: spread the top and sides of a 20cm (8in) round sponge cake with 250g (8oz/2 cups) of buttercream. Smooth the surface with a small palette knife dipped in hot water. Tint some buttercream with a few drops of orange food colouring and fill a nylon piping bag fitted with a small star tube. Pipe alternate inwards and outwards scrolls around the top and bottom edges of the cake. Mark 6.5cm (2½in) circle in the centre using a plain cutter and pipe scrolls around the outside of the marked circle. Pipe groups of three stars of icing at intervals around the side and top of the cake.

Basket Cake: make a quick-mix pudding basin cake (see chart on page 33) flavour 250g (8oz/2 cups) of buttercream with cocoa and spread thinly on the cake, place on a small cake board. Fit a paper piping bag with a basket or ribbon tube and fill with icing. Fold down the top and pipe a basketweave design all around the cake until completely covered. Pipe a shell edging around the base and the top edge using the same piping tube. Fold a 20cm (8in) length of foil into a narrow strip. Wrap 1.5cm (½in) wide ribbon just ovelapping around the strip of foil to cover, then secure the end with tape.

Bend to form a handle, press carefully into the top of the cake and tie a bow on the handle. Fill the centre of the basket with sugar and chocolate eggs, or sugar flowers.

Piping Techniques

Piping Techniques

When piping a celebration cake with royal icing, it is as well to practise before starting on the cake. Make sure the icing is the correct consistency. Use a piping bag fitted with a straight-sided metal tube, as this gives a clean sharp icing result.

Half-fill the bag with icing; do not be tempted to fill it to the top as it is more difficult to squeeze the icing out of a full bag. A good guide to remember is the smaller the icing tube, the less icing you require to work with.

Hold the piping bag comfortably, like a pencil, with the tube through the first two fingers and thumb. Apply the pressure at the top of the bag. Wrists and arms should be relaxed, ready to guide the tube.

Stand or sit comfortably and hold the tube just above the surface of the cake, in an upright position. Press the icing gently on the surface of the cake to form a star. Stop pressing and sharply lift the bag to break off the icing. Pipe another star next to the first one, and continue to pipe the required design.

For piping lines, the tube should be tilted at an angle and a continuous flow of icing should be maintained.
Pipe the beginning of the line on to

the surface of the cake, lift the bag slightly and pipe just above the surface. Allow the line of icing to fall where required before breaking off the thread. See page 101 for instructions on making piped flowers.

Scrolls and Trellis Work

1. Hold a paper piping bag fitted with a star tube at an angle to pipe individual scrolls. Stop pressing the bag and pull off sharply to finish each scroll.

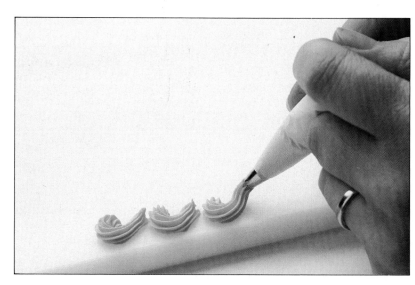

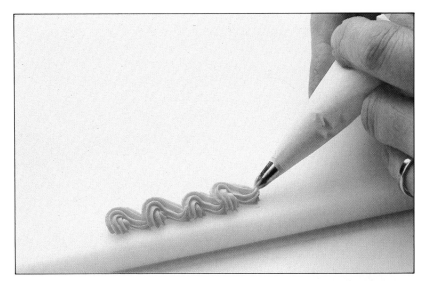

2. Pipe a line of joined-up scrolls.

3. Hold the paper piping bag fitted with a star tube at an angle and pipe a continuous line of icing in a rope design.

4. Use a paper piping bag fitted with a plain writing tube to pipe a lattice or trellis design. Pipe evenly spaced lines of icing, allowing the thread of icing to fall straight.

5. Overpipe threads of icing in the opposite direction to form a lattice or trellis design.

Cornelli Work

1. Fill a paper piping bag with a No 0 or 00 piping tube. Hold your bag between your thumb and first finger using the bag like a pen. Draw a W and M shape with the piping tube keeping up a constant pressure. Work in an erratic pattern not in lines.

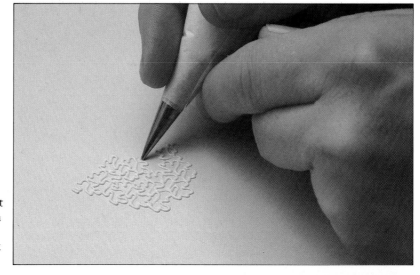

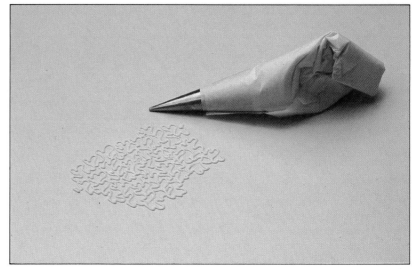

2. Completed cornelli work shown in a contrasting colour but it is equally effective worked in the same colour as the base.

Colours and Tints

The ordinary bottles of liquid colourings available in supermarkets and shops will readily tint or colour icings and frostings in the basic primary colours, and with careful blending other colours and shades can be made.

Moulded and cutout flowers and sugar pieces can now be coloured with blossom tints, or painted with lustre colours when dry. This prevents the risk of colours running into the icing when the atmosphere is damp, and also ensures that the colours will not quickly fade.

Good quality colours are available as pastes, powders and liquids. They are very concentrated and need to be added drop by drop using a cocktail stick to carefully tint the icing to a delicate colour. Remember that food colourings deepen on standing and dry a deeper colour than when first

mixed. Colour icings in the daylight and leave them for at least 15 minutes to assess the colour.

If several batches of coloured icing have to be made, keep some icing in reserve to match the colour correctly. Always remember that a cake should look edible, so keep to pastel shades.

Step-by-Step Simple Flowers

Showing a variety of simply piped flowers using only a paper piping bag snipped into an inverted V.

1. Tint the icing pale mauve and press out a petal shape from the piping bag. Pipe three individual petals with the fourth petal in the centre.

2. Tint the icing pale pink and pipe 5 petals in a circle, then pipe another 3 petals in the centre of the 5 petals, and 2 more petals to finish the flowers.

3. Pipe 5 white petals in a circle. Fill a paper piping bag with yellow icing, and pipe one circle of icing in the centre, then over-pipe with another 2 circles.

4. Tint the icing pale pink and pipe 6 petals in a circle. Fill a paper piping bag with white icing, snip off the point and pipe a swirl of icing in the centre.

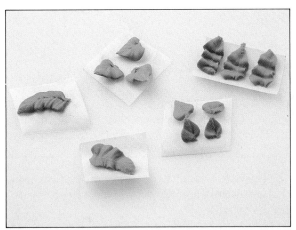

5. Tint the icing green and pipe the icing into short or long leaf shapes.

6. Tint the icing orange, hold the paper piping bag at an angle so it is almost flat with the surface. Pipe the petals flat in a circular movement, bringing the end inwards. Pipe 6 petals in a circle. Use yellow icing to pipe beads of icing in the centre.

7. Tint the icing yellow and pipe 5 petal shapes in a circle. Pipe a circle of orange icing in the centre from a paper piping bag with a tiny end snipped off.

8. Pipe 3 yellow petals in a circle, then pipe 2 more in the centre and pipe the last petal on top.

Simple Flowers Piped with a Petal Tube

1. Using a petal tube with the thick end on the base, pipe a cone. Add more petals around the outside to the required size.

2. Pipe as for the rose bud, adding more petals as required but holding the tube flatter to create more open petals.

3. Holding the petal tube on the side so it is flat, pipe about 12 tiny petals in a circle. Using yellow icing, pipe small beads to fill the centre.

4. Holding the petal tube flat, pipe the petal shape in a circle. Pipe another 2 petals on each side. Pipe the fourth petal to join up the circle. Pipe the last petal the opposite way round in a circle. Pipe yellow threads of icing in the centre.

Simple Piped Flowers

1. To pipe a rose secure a piece of greaseproof or waxed paper to the rose nail with a bead of icing. Pipe the centre using a petal tube on the paper and turning the nail at the same time to form a cone shape. Keep the piping tube upright and the thick end of the tube at the base.

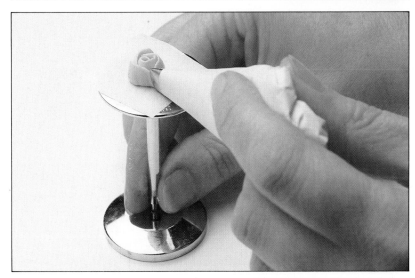

2. Pipe the third petal around the centre petals turning the nail at the same time as pressing the bag.

3. Hold the piping bag at an angle to pipe the final petals. To pipe a rose bud, start with the centre cone, then pipe around more petals until the bud is the size required.

Simple Lettering on a Plaque

1. Trace the letters onto a piece of clean greaseproof or waxed paper. Place the tracing over the sugarpaste plaque and mark out each letter.

2. Using a filled paper piping bag fitted with a No 1 writing tube, pipe the outline of each letter. Stop pressing the piping bag halfway through each letter to prevent the icing piping on.

3. HAPPY BIRTHDAY piped on the plaque.

Simple Decorations

Once the cake has been marzipanned and iced, it is ready to be piped according to the design you have chosen. Always choose a simple design at first with simple piping; do not attempt too much, otherwise the result may be very disappointing.

Think carefully about the design and the colour of the cake. Cut out a paper template and transfer the design by pricking through or around the template with a pin onto the surface of the cake. Pipe the design using only one or two different piping tubes. Mark the design onto the side of the cake and repeat the piping to match the top, or tie ribbon around instead.

Add some simple sugar flowers and leaves, which may be piped in advance and stored. Most of them require just the paper piping bag trimmed to an inverted V.

Pink and White Wedding Cake: make a 25cm (10in) round and a 20cm (8in) round rich or light fruit cake or madeira cake, marzipanned and royal iced. Cut two paper circles each 5cm (2in) smaller than the top of each cake. Fold each circle in half, then fold the half circle twice more to form a cone shape. Place an upturned cup on the wide end of each cone and draw an arc shape around the outside of the cup. Using a pair of sharp scissors, cut out the arc shape to make a scallop. Open the template and place the larger size on the large cake. Mark around the template using a pin to transfer the design to the cake top.

Half-fill a bag fitted with a No 1 plain tube. Use white royal icing. Pipe a thread of icing from each point of the design. Repeat to pipe a second line 1.5cm (½in) outside the first scalloped design, then overpipe with pink icing using the same piping tube. Pipe short trailing threads of icing towards the top edge and base of the cake, keeping the thread touching the surface.

Pipe seven white beads of icing on each thread of icing nearest to the board and overpipe with pink beads. Use 16 simple pink sugar flowers and secure 8 on top of the cake with a little icing opposite each point. Secure the remaining 8 flowers to the end of each thread of icing on the side of the cake. Using a piping bag filled

with white royal icing, snip into an inverted V and pipe leaves in groups around the side of the cake. Using a medium-sized star tube, pipe a star border around the top and bottom edges of the cake and leave to dry.

Repeat the same design on the

smaller cake. Trim the cake boards with white ribbon and support the top cake with three white cake pillars. Make an arrangement of silk flowers to go on top of the cake, secured with white marzipan or sugarpaste, or fill a small vase with silk or fresh flowers.

Icing Runouts

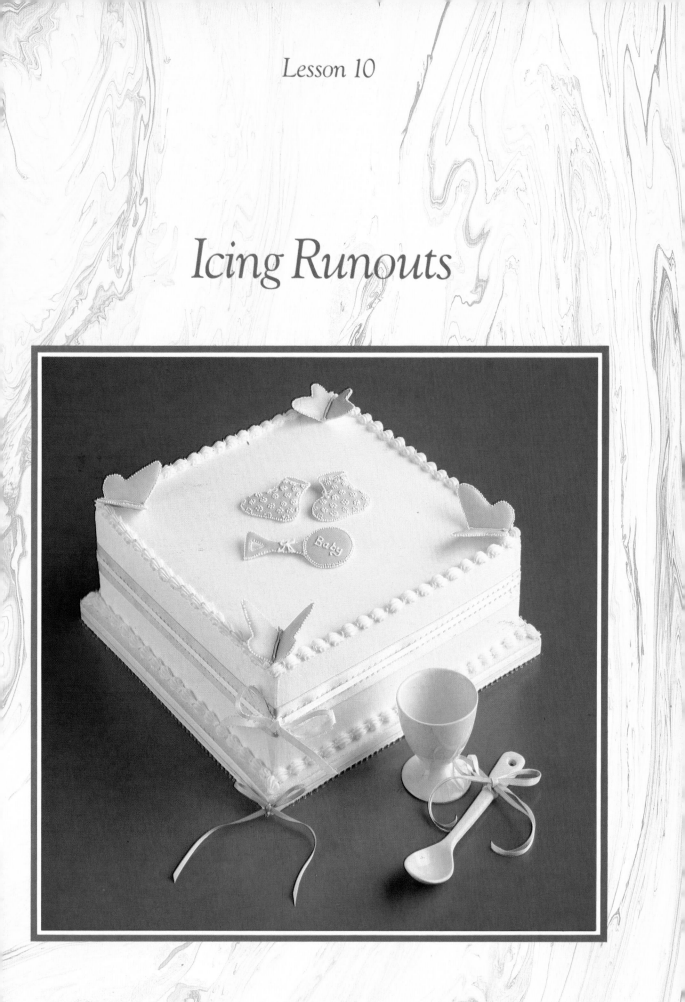

Icing Runouts

Make simple runout shapes to decorate a variety of cakes. Choose bold shapes at first with one outline, then try some more complicated shapes. Icing consistency is very important, and do have everything ready

The consistency and texture of the royal icing must be right or the runouts will be difficult to make and handle. Use double strength dried egg albumen or egg whites with no additives such as glycerine or lemon juice. The icing should be light and glossy, not heavy and dull. When the spoon is lifted, a soft peak should form which will bend at the tip. This is the consistency required for piping the outline of the runouts. If the icing thread keeps breaking, it is because the consistency is too stiff or the icing has not been made correctly: too much sugar added too quickly and not enough mixing.

Icing to fill in the runout must be soft enough to flow with the aid of a paintbrush, just holding its shape until tapped, then becoming smooth.

Leave the icing to stand for at least 2 hours or overnight if possible, covered with damp muslin (cheesecloth), allowing any air bubbles to come to the surface. Tap the bowl several times until there are no more bubbles.

Once made, runouts can be kept successfully between layers of waxed or greaseproof paper in a box stored in a dry place. This means a quantity of runouts can be made in advance, allowing more time to flat ice and pipe the cake.

Runouts are very fragile so it is wise to choose a solid shape at first, and make more than required to allow for breakages. When you are confident about making simple, small, solid shapes, practise making finer pieces, figures and scenes. Accuracy, not

speed, is important when making runouts, so allow plenty of time.

EQUIPMENT

Good quality double sided waxed paper is best for tracing the design or shape on, and being fine it does not wrinkle as the runouts dry. If using single sided use the shiny side face up. For larger, more solid, runouts, non-stick baking parchment (paper) may be used instead. Pencil, fine paintbrush, cocktail stick, needle, paper piping bags, No 0 or piping tube. Royal icing, edible food colours, a board or tray on which to put runouts while they are being piped.

Making an Icing Runout

Royal Icing runouts are one of the most useful forms of cake decoration. They can be made in any shape or form by simply tracing over a chosen design or pattern.

Draw or trace the chosen design several times on a piece of paper, spaced well apart. Secure the paper to a flat surface with sticky tape or dots of icing. Cover the design with a piece of waxed paper and secure with four or six dots of icing.

Fit a paper piping bag with a No 0 tube and half-fill with icing to pipe the outline. Fill another paper piping bag with soft icing.

Pipe carefully around the outline with as few breaks as possible; a small runout can be piped with one continuous thread of icing. Squeeze out a little icing at an unobtrusive point of the runout and secure the icing thread. Lift the thread of icing just above the surface and squeeze the bag gently following the outline of the tracing, and allowing the thread to fall on the marked line around the shape of the runout. Stop squeezing to prevent the icing thread from running on, and join the icing at the point where it started.

Snip the pointed end off the soft icing bag and fill in the runout. Start by piping around the inside edge to keep the outline soft, otherwise it may break, and work towards the centre. Fill the shape so that the icing looks rounded and full.

Using a fine paintbrush, needle or cocktail stick, ensure the area is completely covered and the icing is smooth. Gently tap the board so that any air bubbles rise to the surface; if so, break these with a pin.

Carefully remove the waxed paper and runout from the template and leave to dry. Cover the drawing design with more waxed paper and repeat to make as many runouts and spares as required.

Leave the runouts to dry in a warm, dry place overnight until they set hard. The more quickly they dry, the glossier they will be. Carefully peel off the paper from the runout and store runouts in a box between layers of waxed paper.

Arrange runouts on the cake and secure with small dots of icing.

Christening Cake

Christening Cake:
Make a 20cm (8in) square rich or light fruit cake or Madeira cake. Marzipan and flat ice with royal icing.

Make four pairs of butterfly wings, a pair of booties, and a rattle runouts, tracing from the template and following the instructions. Make a few extra of each in case of breakages. Use pale blue icing.

When completely dry, carefully remove the runouts from the paper and half-fill a paper piping bag, fitted with a No 0 plain piping tube, with white royal icing.

Pipe tiny beads of icing all around the edge of each runout and pipe circles of beads around a centre bead of icing all over the booties to represent tiny flowers. Pipe threads of icing into bows on the booties and rattle, and pipe BABY across the centre of the rattle. Leave to dry.

Using a paper piping bag fitted with a medium-sized star tube, half-filled with white royal icing, pipe a shell border around the top edge and base of the cake. Pipe a star of icing on the back of the booties and rattle and place on the centre of the cake. Pipe a line of white icing at each corner and press the butterfly wings in position. Half-fill a paper piping bag fitted with a No 1 tube with blue icing. Pipe a thread down the centre of each butterfly, with two beads on the end. Pipe blue beads of icing in between each shell and leave to dry.
(See photograph on page 107)

Bootie Runout

1. The runout shape drawn on a piece of paper with waxed paper ready to cover the drawing.

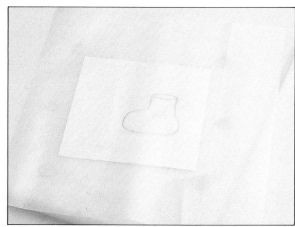

2. The waxed paper over the runout drawing held in position by beads of icing.

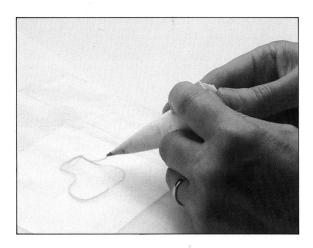

3. Using a number 0 plain piping tube and royal icing, pipe the outline of the runout with one continuous thread of icing.

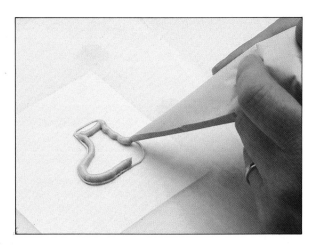

4. Fill in the runout with pale blue royal icing starting at the edges and working inwards.

5. The runout completely filled in with royal icing.

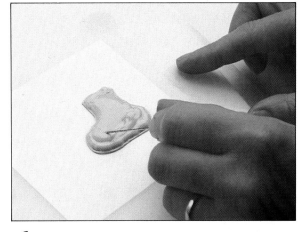

6. Use a pin to level the surface of the icing runout.

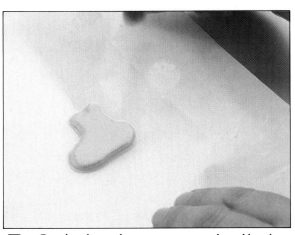

7. Gently vibrate the runout to smooth and level the icing and encourage any air bubbles to rise to the surface.

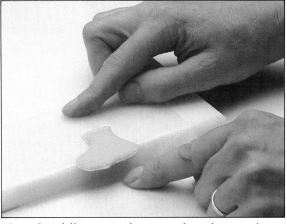

8. Carefully remove the runout from the paper by resting the runout on the edge of a board and pulling the waxed paper away from underneath.

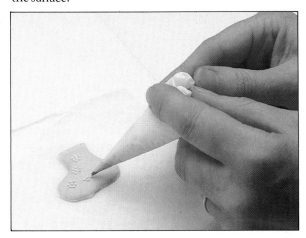

9. Using the outlining tube to pipe beads of icing on to the runout into a tiny flower pattern.

10. Pipe beads of icing around the outside edge of the runout.

Rattle Runout

1. The runout shape drawn on a piece of paper with a piece of waxed paper ready to cover the outline drawing.

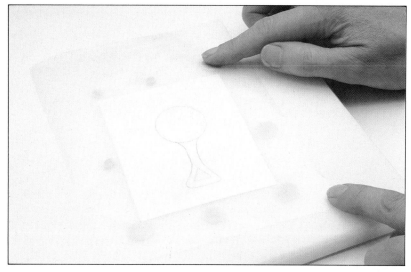

2. The runout drawing covered with waxed paper and held in position by pressing on to the beads of icing ready for piping.

3. Use a number 0 plain piping tube and royal icing, pipe the outline of the runout with one continuous thread of icing.

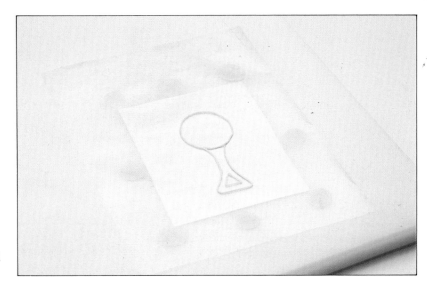

4. The runout completely outlined with a thread of royal icing.

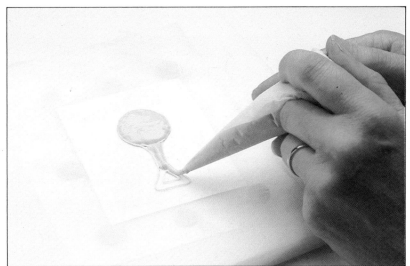

5. The round part of the runout filled in with pale blue royal icing and piping in the handle.

6. Use a pin to level the surface of the icing runout.

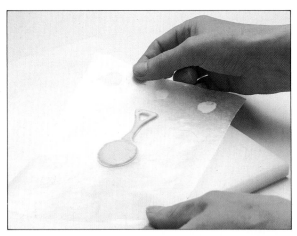

7. Gently vibrate the runout to smooth and level the icing and encourage any air bubbles to rise to the surface.

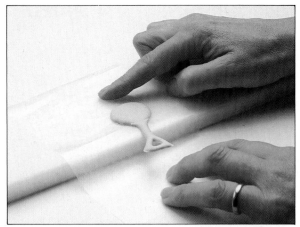

8. Carefully remove the runout from the paper by resting the runout on the edge of a board and pulling the waxed paper away from underneath.

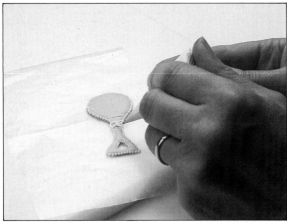

9. The runout outline piped with beads of icing from the number 0 tube. Pipe a tiny bow from one thread of icing.

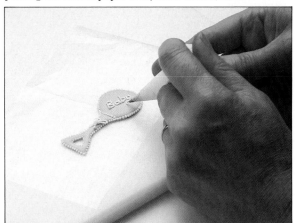

10. Pipe the word BABY in the centre of the runout.

Ribbons in Cake Decorating

Ribbons in Cake Decorating

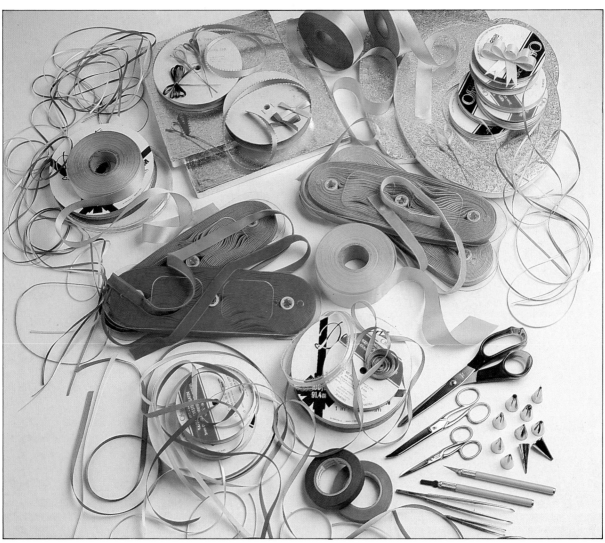

Choosing ribbons

Specialist shops and department stores offer an enormous variety of ribbons made from paper, nylon, polyester acetate and velvet. Each one has many different uses, but the type most commonly used is double-faced polyester satin with woven edges. This has an attractive sheen and will not fray. It is available in widths from 15mm to 2.5cm (¹⁄₁₆-1in), in over one hundred colours. Double-faced polyester satin is used for loops and bows in flower sprays, ribbon insertion and banding, and in all kinds of top and side decorations.

Nylon ribbon comes in a large range of colours and sizes, but it is really suitable only for banding boards or cakes. Nylon ribbons are unsuitable for bows and loops as they are too limp to hold a shape. To test whether a ribbon is suitable for loops, take a piece and fold it over. If it supports its weight, then it will look attractive. A ribbon that goes limp will produce flat, messy bows.

Velvet ribbon is rich looking but heavy, so it is usually used only for cake boards. Occasionally, narrow velvet ribbons are used as loops and trailers in sprays.

Paper and synthetic fabric ribbons, including filigree ribbons and metalic twine found in gift wrap departments, can also be used to great effect. Filigree ribbons are delicate in sprays, and look pretty around cake boards, particularly when combined with narrow satin ribbons.

116

Ribbons are certainly the most widely used nonedible decoration in sugarcraft. As well as being used in all flower sprays and arrangements, ribbons are used to cover cake boards, band cakes, make pictures or designs on the top or side of a cake, or to decorate an entire cake, as in the Maypole Cake on page 126.

Ribbon collages

These simple, colourful designs are quick and easy to create and require no special skills. The ribbons can be positioned directly on the top or sides of a cake, or on a prepared sugarpaste plaque. Choose a simple design, such as the ones shown here, and draw it on paper. Cut different lengths of ribbon and place it on the design. Transfer the ribbons to the cake or plaque, fixing them with a little royal icing. The easiest way to do this is to paint the royal icing on the back of the ribbon with a fine paintbrush.

Make this sailboat collage with a ribbon flower made from 5mm (¼in) satin ribbon, and a sailboat cut from different widths of satin ribbon. Bands of narrow ribbon can be used to finish the collage. Add miniature bows in matching colours.

Ribbons of different textures and widths are used to make this pretty strawberry basket. To weave the basket, fix the light coloured ribbons in place, then thread the dark ribbons through them fixing with dots of icing. Add the curved handle, then fill the basket with flowers, leaves and red strawberries. Pipe tiny dots of white royal icing for the seeds.

Ribbon Insertion

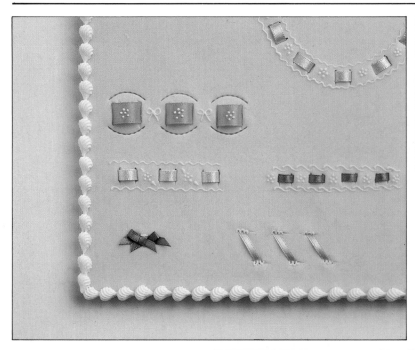

Ribbon insertion is a technique to create the effect that a single piece of ribbon has been threaded or woven through the icing. It is usually done on sugarpaste, although it can also be attractive on a marzipan-covered or royal-iced cake. The designs can be straight, diagonal or curved, and are often combined with crimper work.

The sugarpaste should be skinned, (ie,it should have dried to form a thin crust, but not be set hard). Plan the design on paper first, then use pins or a scriber to transfer it to the cake. Choose ribbon of the required width, and cut as many pieces as necessary to make the design. The pieces should be slightly longer than the spaces, leaving enough at each end to tuck in.

Use a very fine-bladed sharp knife, such as a craft knife or scalpel, to cut slits in the sugarpaste. Use the ribbon insertion blade or a pin to tuck the ribbon into the slits. It should stay in place without fixing.

Finish off the ribbon insertion with miniature bows and piped embroidery designs, if wished. If the ribbon is wide enough, tiny flowerrs can be piped on each piece.

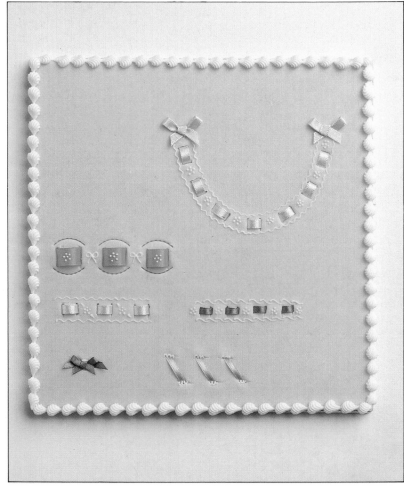

Banding Cake Boards

Any kind of ribbon can be used to cover the cake board. Choose colours which combine or contrast with the colours of the cake. It is usual to pin the ribbons onto the board, do not use glue, which may stain the ribbon, or give off toxic fumes.

1. Hold the board firmly and use a long, flat-headed pin to attach the ribbon in position.

2. Stretch the ribbon tightly around the board. If the board is large it may be necessary to use more pins or dabs of royal icing to keep the ribbon from slipping. Pin in place at the join.

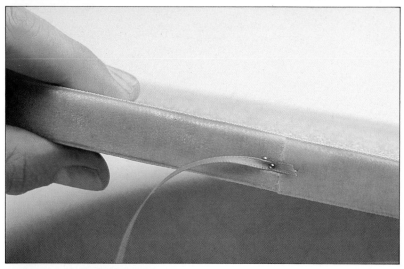

3. Cut the ribbon evenly. If adding a contrasting band, pin over the join and stretch the ribbon around the board as for the first one.

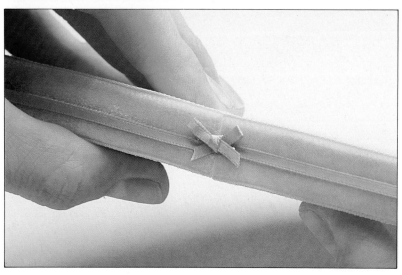

4. Pin the second ribbon and trim neatly. Finish off the board by pinning a small bow over the join.

Floristry Ribbon

Floristry ribbon is made from shiny paper, and it is used in commercial bouquets and in gift wrapping. It is very inexpensive, and it can be used in cake decorating to band boards, for ribbon collages, and for simple curled designs.

1. Cut the ribbon into lengths of about 60cm (24in). Hold it tightly to stop if from curling up.

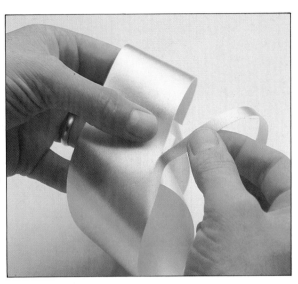

2. Hold one side of the ribbon and tear it in strips, starting at the top of the other side. It should tear evenly into about ten narrow strips.

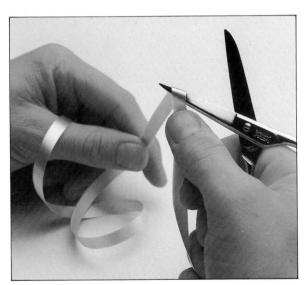

3. To curl the ribbon, run the blade of a pair of scissors down the length. The curls could be used on the Maypole Cake.

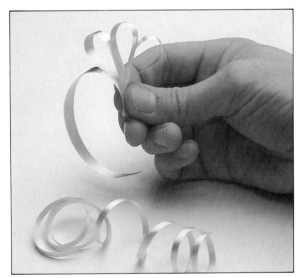

4. The strips can be made into loops and used as fillers in fabric flower arrangements. Fasten with royal icing.

Miniature Bows

Tiny bows are used in many different ways on cakes. They can decorate the sides of a plainly iced cake, placed above frills and flounces, used in runout, embroidery and broderie anglaise designs, or placed on

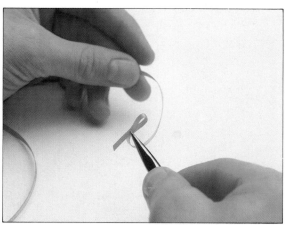

1. Hold the ribbon in one hand and make a loop with a small tail in the end. Hold the loop with the tweezers.

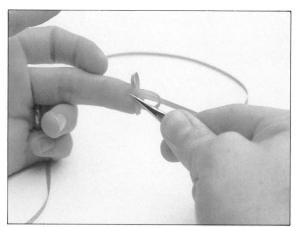

2. Take the length of ribbon around the tweezers, making a complete circle. There should be two small loops.

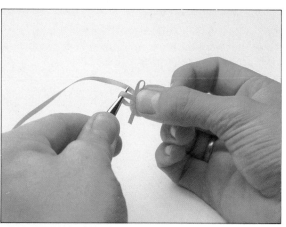

3. Hold the loops with your fingers and release the tweezers. Put the tweezers through the loop and pull through the ribbon from the other side.

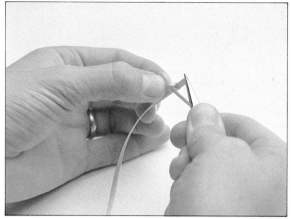

4. Use the tweezers to pull the loops tight and ensure that they are the same size.

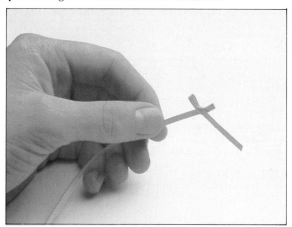

5. When the bow is tight, cut the tails evenly. Save the trimmings to use for ribbon insertion.

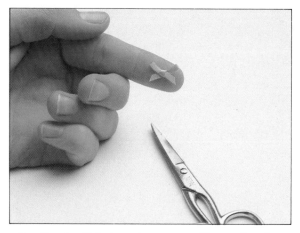

6. Finish off the bows by cutting a V in each tail, or by trimming neatly on the diagonal.

top of bells, horseshoes or other top decorations. **The bows must be tied so that they will lie flat. Larger bows can be tied with your fingers, but tweezers are necessary for very tiny ones.**

1. Miniature bows in an assortment of colours.

2. Two-colour miniature bows.

3. Larger bows which can be made without the use of tweezers.

4. Make as for the double loop, but fold the ends of the ribbon and bring these up to make the tails.

5. Single loops fixed with royal icing. Decorate with tiny piped or fabric flowers.

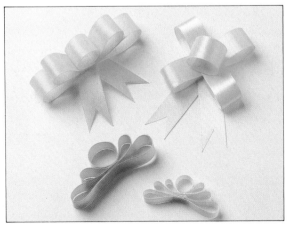

6. Ribbon loop bows. These can be made from any width of fabric or paper ribbon. Fix in position with royal icing.

Wired Ribbons

The loops and bows shown here are all for use in floral bouquets and sprays. They are all made with floristry wire, usually 28-gauge, so that they can then be wired into the

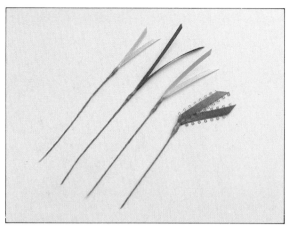

Swallow tail: Fold a piece of ribbon in half. Take a length of wire and wrap it round the fold of the ribbon several times, then bend the wire down and cover with tape. Trim the ribbon ends to points.

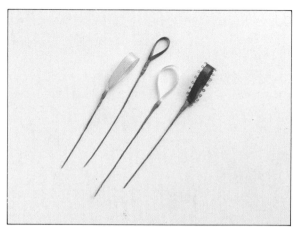

Single loop: Make a ribbon loop and wrap floristry wire tightly around the ends. Cover the join and the length of wire with tape.

Double loop: Make two ribbon loops of equal size and join with wire. Cover the join and the wire with tape.

Triple loop: Make three equal-sized ribbon loops, wrap floristry wire tightly around the joins, and cover the join and wire with tape.

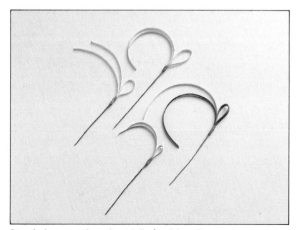

Single loop with tails: Make a ribbon loop, then bring the ends up to make two long tails, or trailers. Bind the wire tightly around the fold, then cover with wire.

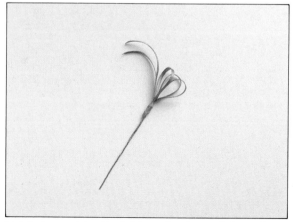

Triple loop with tails: Make as for the triple loop, but fold the ends of the ribbon and bring up to make the tails, which can be long or short, curled or straight.

sprays. For a simple and unusual decoration, place a bunch of ribbon loops in a small vase, or combine the loops with fabric flowers. Never place the wires directly into the cake.

Figure-of-eight: Take a length of ribbon in one hand and bring it round your hand so that it lies flat. Make three more loops, changing direction each time. Bind with wire where the points of the loops meet. Trim the ends of the ribbon.

Wired bows: Fold a length of ribbon into three equal pieces, then wrap a piece of wire around the centre. Trim the ends to make a bow shape.

Double wired bows: These can be made with several loops. Fold the ribbon as for the single bow as many times as required, wire in the centre and trim the ends.

Maypole Cake

U se the ribbon-making techniques you have mastered to make this delightful Maypole Cake. Although the design is very simple, it is effective and appealing.

If the cake has not already been marzipaned on a board, centre the cake on the board. Evenly spread the top with the green icing, then use the flat side of the palette knife to bring up tiny peaks to look like grass. Place the cake on a turntable and evenly spread the sides of the cake with white icing, then pull on icing comb evenly around the sides to make the wavy lines. Spread the board with green icing as for the top. Cover the piece of dowelling with ribbons, fix them with dabs of royal icing, and insert the pole into the centre of the cake before the icing sets. Fill a small bag with a No 3 tube with white icing. Pip dots of icing around the top and base of the cake and quickly attach the sugarpaste flowers. Position some flowers around the base of the pole. Pipe green leaves above and below the flowers with a No 67 tube or snipped paper piping bag. Make six bows and attach around the sides of the cake. Cut each ribbon in half and fasten to the top fo the Maypole with a pin. Pin a miniature bow at the top. Cover the cake board with the three ribbon bands and pin in place.

EQUIPMENT
30cm (12in) round cake board
20cm (8in) piece of wooden dowelling, ribbon to cover the dowelling
2m (2yd) 5mm (¼in) ribbon, in each of pink, peach and lemon
1m (1yd) 5mm (¼in) ribbon in each of dark pink, yellow and mauve for covering the board.
flat-headed pins
Pallette knife
Icing comb
Piping tube No 3
Leaf tube No 67

Time
2 hours

INGREDIENTS
20cm (8in) round fruit cake, covered with marzipan
or
20cm (8in) round, firm sponge cake, sandwiched with jam and lightly covered with buttercream
450g (1lb) pale green royal icing
450g (1lb) white royal icing
approximately 100 sugarpaste plunger-cutter flowers in pale pink, dark pink and lemon.

VARIATION
The sides of the cake can be covered with ribbon bands to match the streamers, instead of the rings of flowers.

Designing a Cake

Designing a Cake

The design of a cake is most important. When decorating a cake you should have a mental picture of what the cake will look like when it is finished.

The design of the cake begins before you even bake the cake and is broken down into several main areas.

Shape and Design

Nowadays there are so many different shaped cake tins available that it is sometimes a difficult decision to make to decide on the shape. Often at this stage you will have to sit down with a sketch pad and draw various cake shapes, then work out the basic design. If a spray of flowers is the focal point, decide on the shape of the spray. This may give an idea of the shape of cake it will suit. For a runout motif, see what shape it suggests.

These are all important factors, as a cake should look evenly balanced with not too many bare areas. Sometimes if you are commissioned to decorate a cake you will be given some idea of colour, shape or design. This gives a base upon which to plan your design and makes the overall design a lot easier to work out. If no instructions are given, try and find out favourite colours, flowers, hobbies and pastimes of the person the cake is for. This can spark off the imagination and may provide a theme for the cake design.

Once the shape has been decided upon think about the size. This again

is very important, especially when designing a wedding cake. It would be silly to make a 30cm (12in) birthday cake if only 15-20 portions were required, as a 20cm (8in) cake would be more than enough. The other extreme would be a 13, 18, 23cm (5, 7, 9in) wedding cake made if 450 portions were required. With a wedding cake it is traditional to keep the top tier for the first anniversary or the christening of the first child. This means that enough portions should be got out of the bottom tier/s. An additional cutting cake can also be made. This is a cake iced but not decorated.

128

Base Colour and Covering Medium

The colour of the base of the cake has to be a well thought out decision, as it can dramatically alter the finished effect of the cake. There are two main choices of covering medium: royal icing or sugarpaste. Both give different effects. Royal icing, with its sharp precise angles, gives a more formal effect and sugarpaste, with its soft rounded edges giving a more feminine effect. A few years ago all wedding cakes were covered in white; nowadays white cakes have taken second place to pastel shades. The covering looks more attractive if it is a pale colour, but not too pale as very pale pastels look washed out or dirty, and do not make too dark, as it will look too harsh once decorated. Remember most colours dry slightly darker, so take this into consideration when colouring the icing.

Main Design

Once the cake is covered you can then move onto the main decoration. Designs can be copied straight out of a book, if you find it difficult to design, or look through your books and take different parts from different cakes. For example, you may like an embroidery design from one cake and a spray of flowers from another, and so on.

If you are putting runout collars on a cake you will have to design these. If you are putting on frills or lace you will have to make templates to ensure correct positioning.

The overall design of the cake can be made up of lots of ideas, favourite colours, flowers, hobbies, designs taken from wedding stationary, the wedding dress or veil, a christening robe, etc. Inspiration can also be taken from nature. Often on a country walk you will see something that could work well in icing.

It is better to under-decorate and it is not necessary to use all the skills and techniques you have learnt on one cake. Your skill as a decorator will improve if you try new designs all the time rather than sticking to one or two favourite designs. Although you will become quicker if your repeat a design over and over again, you will also become stale and get little satisfaction from your cakes. There is nothing nicer than to design and decorate a cake then to stand back and think you created the whole thing from your mind and hands. Many cake designs, especially patterns for runouts, collars and plaques involve the use of geometry because accuracy is of vital importance.

Drawing Geometric Templates

Here a 10cm (4in) circle drawn with compasses, shows the radius. This is the straight line drawn from the centre point to disect any point on the outer line. This line is known as the circumference.

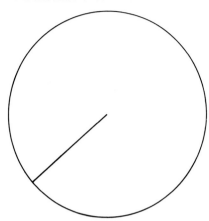

The same circle showing the diameter. This line crosses from one side of the circle to the other at any angle, but should go through the centre point.

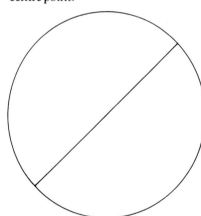

The radius of a circle disects the circumference into six equal parts.

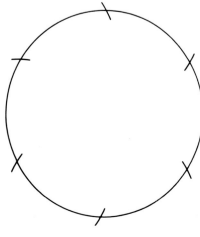

Hold the compass from the centre to the outer edge, mark the edge and then place the needle on the mark and mark in front where it crosses again. Continue all the way around until you have six marks on the circumference.

Here the six points have been joined with six straight lines to make a perfect hexagon. This principle is ideal for drawing hexagonal plaques and boards.

The circle with its six marks can also be used to make a triangle by only using three of the six points.

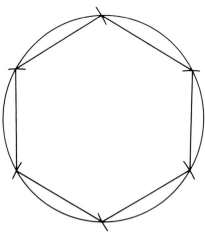

Portions from a Cake
The chart gives a rough idea of how many portions you would get out of a particular size cake. The calculations have been based on catering portions. Some caterers will cut 2.5cm (1in) squares, others 1cm x 5cm (½in x 2in) slices. It is always better to over estimate the number of portions required.

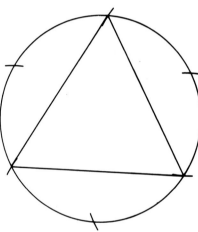

Portions

Round	Portions	Square	Portions
13cm (5in)	14	13cm (5in)	16
15cm (6in)	22	15cm (6in)	27
18cm (7in)	30	18cm (7in)	40
20cm (8in)	40	20cm (8in)	54
23cm (9in)	54	23cm (9in)	70
25cm (10in)	68	25cm (10in)	90
27.5cm (11in)	86	27.5cm (11in)	112
30cm (12in)	100	30cm (12in)	134

At a glance Wedding Cake Portions)	(Portions for Total Cake)	
	Round	Square
3-Tier Small 13, 18, 23cm (5, 7, 9in)	98	126
3-Tier Large 15, 20, 25cm (6, 8, 10in)	130	171
2-Tier Standard 18 and 25cm (7 and 10in)	98	130

Note
You can also make an additional cutting cake if more portions are required. The other shapes such as heart, hexagonal, octagonal and petal will give approximately the same portions as a round cake of the same size.

*The design sketch for the blue
birthday cake featured at the
beginning of this chapter, showing
top and side elevation.*

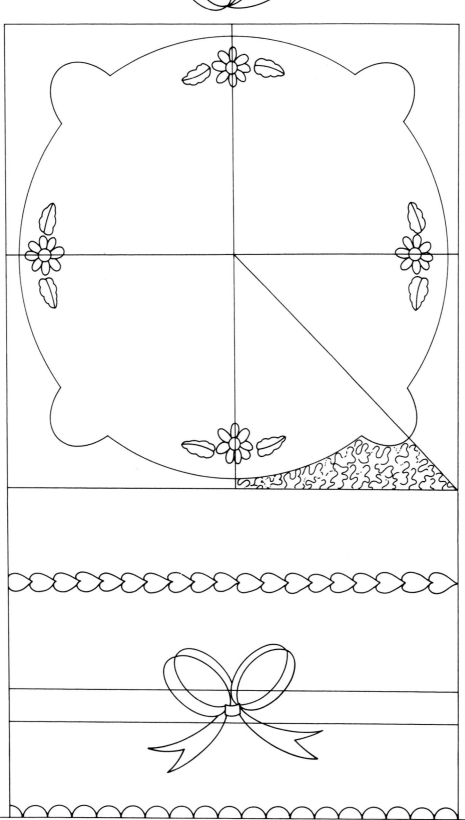

Americans excel at pressure piping, with beautiful cakes decorated completely in pressure piping. Flowers piped flat on flowers nails are popular. Gum paste (pastillage) is used for cake ornaments, figures and boxes for candies.

Australia

The Australian style of work has now become very popular worldwide, with many people taking courses in the types of techniques used in Australia.

Australians cover cakes with sugarpaste, never with royal icing which is only used for piping. They excel in fine piping techniques, such as embroidery, lace and extension work. A decorator may spend weeks on one lace extension border around a cake. Sugar flowers are also popular. The warm climate produces exotic flowers and cakes often feature the Australian wild flowers.

South Africa

The warm climate in South Africa produces beautiful flowers, and sugar flowers feature in the cake decorating. The flowers are almost always the main focal point of a cake. The basic cake is usually quite simply decorated to show off the beautiful, imaginative sprays of flowers.

Another South African technique which is now used all over the world is the Garrett frill. This original idea came from Elaine Garrett of Cape Town, although there are now many adaptations of the basic principle.

Filigree work is another technique used in South Africa, cobweb-fine pieces in the form of wings and top ornaments are often added to the cakes.

England

The English are famous for their royal icing techniques which first became popular in Victorian times. However, English decorators have now incorporated styles from Australia and South Africa, and the English style is now quite international.

The World of Cakes

Designs vary throughout the world due to national decorating styles and techniques. A few years ago this was very apparent, as each country had its own style of work, but now with books on techniques available everywhere, cake decorating has become international.

America

Americans rarely use fruit cakes and are famous for their sponge-type cakes which they use for celebrations, covered with frostings in every conceivable colour and flavour. A lot of English cake decorators frown on Americans' choice of colours but forget that colours can to be used with more imagination. Colour has a lot to do with the climate. Most weddings and celebrations throughout the world are held outside, and with the sun shining, bright colours seem much more appropriate.

The range of American tubes is vast, with tubes to pipe every imaginable design and shape.

Designs for runouts, collars and plaques are first cut from paper templates

Create simple side designs by cutting interesting shapes along the flat edge of icing scrapers. These are particularly effective on buttercream cakes.

Side designs may combine a geometric shape and piped ornamentation.

Scroll designs

Scrolls are a common feature in cake design, they are simple to pipe once the basic scroll shape has been mastered.

Designing, Covering and Choosing Cake Boards

Designing Cake Boards

The board the cake sits on is as important as the cake itself. As with the design of a cake, the choice of board starts at the initial stages of planning. Originally, only round and square boards were available, then came heart-shaped and hexagonal boards and more recently manufacturers have started producing boards to match every tin shape. You can also make your own boards for an unusual cake. The picture below shows a variety of cake pillars used for assembling tiered cakes to complete your design.

Shape and Size

The board that you choose does not always have to be the same shape as the cake, for instance, a round cake can look attractive on a petal-shaped board. It all depends on the effect that you want to achieve. Most of the unusual cake boards come in three or four sizes to match the size of the tins. This is fine for most designs, however, if you are planning runout collars you may find that the collar will extend beyond the board. In this case, it is preferable to make the board yourself.

The basic guideline for the size of board is that the board should be 5cm (2in) larger than the cake. The bottom tier of a wedding cake or any cake with a collar should have a board 7.5cm (3in) larger. On wedding cakes it is important not to overshadow the cakes, so the chosen board should not be larger than the cake on that is on the tier below.

Some manufacturers still make boards to the imperial standard of a half inch. Metric boards are slightly

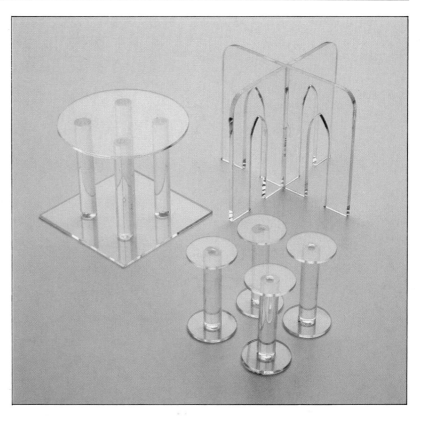

thicker at 2cm. When making a tiered cake, be sure to use boards of the same thickness throughout. If the boards are to be trimmed with ribbon bands, these should also be of the same thickness.

Fruit cakes should always go on 2cm (½in) thick drum cake boards or wooden boards to take the weight of the cake. The other boards, known as double-thick and single-thick cards are only suitable for sponge or novelty cakes.

Jigsaw Boards

Unusual and substantial cake boards may be cut with a jig-saw and made to your own design from 2cm (½in) thick wood or wood-vaneered chipboard. These may then be left plain for some novelty designs decorating the sides with ribbon, or they may be covered to complement the iced cake. The templates at the end of this chapter provide many design ideas.

Covering
Cake Boards

You can cover purchased or made boards with various papers and fabrics to create a special look for each cake. For instance, at Christmas it is attractive to cover the board with red foil or coloured wrapping paper for a seasonal look.

Use laundry starch or cornflour (cornstarch) to stick the paper or foil to the boards. Place a little powdered starch or cornflour (cornstarch) in a small saucepan, add a little water and mix into a smooth paste, thin the paste with a little more water. Bring to the boil then add more water to dilute the glue which at this stage should be quite runny. Use immediately; if the glue cools and thickens, reheat as the glue sticks better when hot. A rubber-based glue is suitable for sticking fabrics.

Covering the Board
Using the board as a template, outline the shape onto the back of the covering paper using a pencil. Draw the outline again this time adding a 5cm (2in) border. Cut out both shapes. Brush hot glue over the top surface of the board, turn the board upsidedown and position centrally on the larger piece of paper. Spread some glue over the edges of the board and a little on the underside. Pull the excess paper over the sides smoothing as you work. On a square board work opposite side together. Make sure the paper is completely stuck down then spread some more glue over the underside of the board. Stick the small piece of paper over the bottom. Sometimes small lumps and air bubbles will be visible but, just like with wallpaper, these should disappear on drying.

Covering the Board with Royal Icing
When coating a cake or even a dummy in royal icing it is usual to coat the board as well. The board will require at least two coats of icing, to achieve a smooth finish and to prevent the icing from splintering.

Covering the Board with Sugarpaste
To cover a board in sugarpaste, follow the principles for making sugarpaste plaques. The board is covered at the same time as the cake and both are left to dry for two to three days. If the cake is placed on the soft paste you are liable to damage the board covering when trying to centre the cake on the board.

Royal Iced Board

1. The cake has received two coats of icing and is thoroughly dried. Now move onto the board. Using royal icing and a palette knife pat the icing onto the board. With the side of the knife, continue all the way around the board.

2. Hold the palette knife flat on the surface of the board and rotate the cake starting and finishing at the seam at the back of the cake.

3. Holding the knife at right angles to the board, rotate the cake to remove excess icing.

4. Rotate the cake again, this time holding the knife at a slight angle to remove the sharp edge from the board coating. On certain designs the edge of the board is relied upon for supporting the hands and an angled edge tends to splinter easily.

Sugarpasted Board

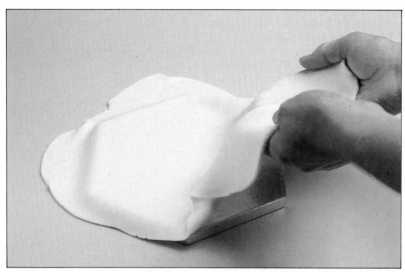

1. Roll out the sugarpaste in the required colour to 5mm (⅛in) thick. Lift up and drape across the board.

2. Cut off the excess paste using a palatte knife, taking care to keep the edge straight.

3. The finished board covered with sugarpaste is left to dry thoroughly before the sugarpasted cake is positioned.

The following templates provide the patterns for the jigsaw boards illustrated in this chapter. Many of the patterns represent half the completed board, the remainder are shown whole. Size up or down as required.

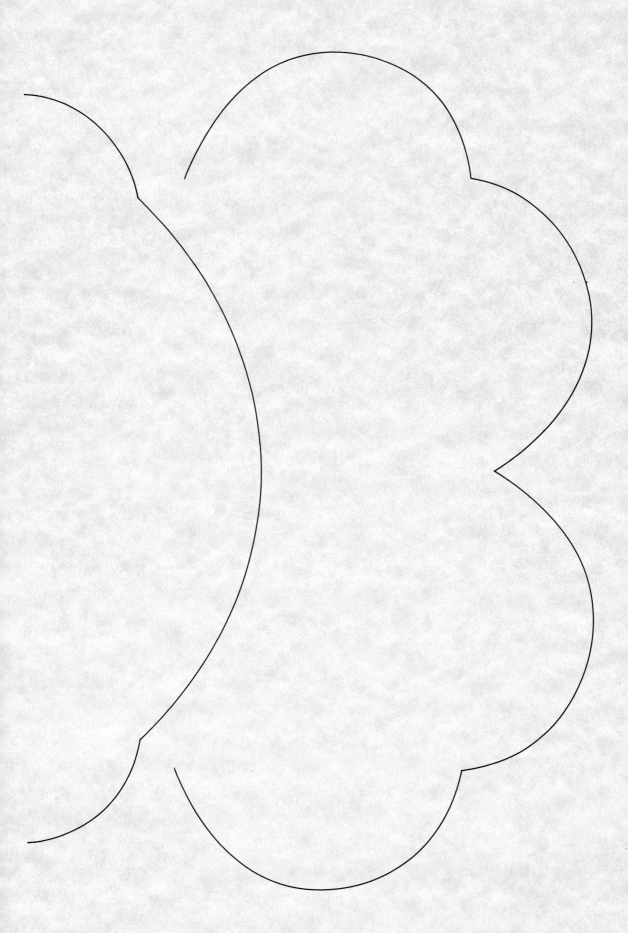

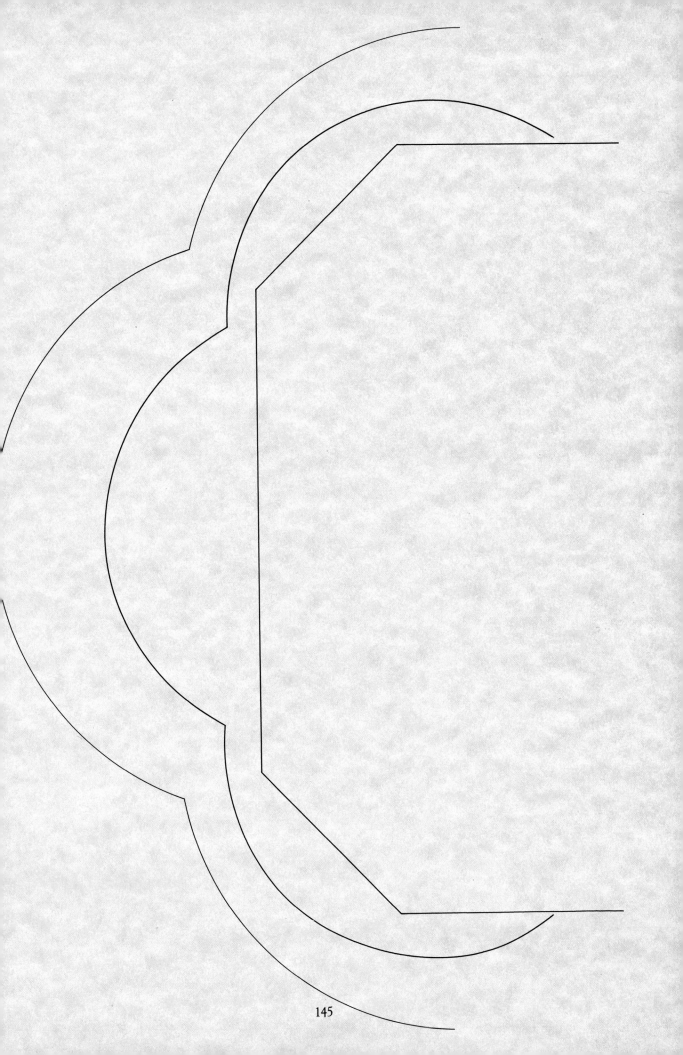

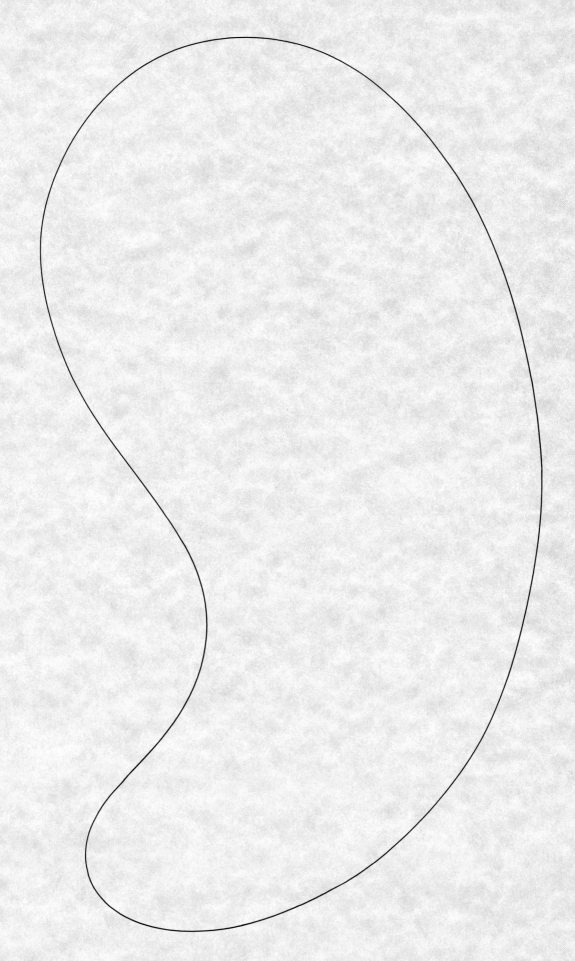

Sugar Moulding

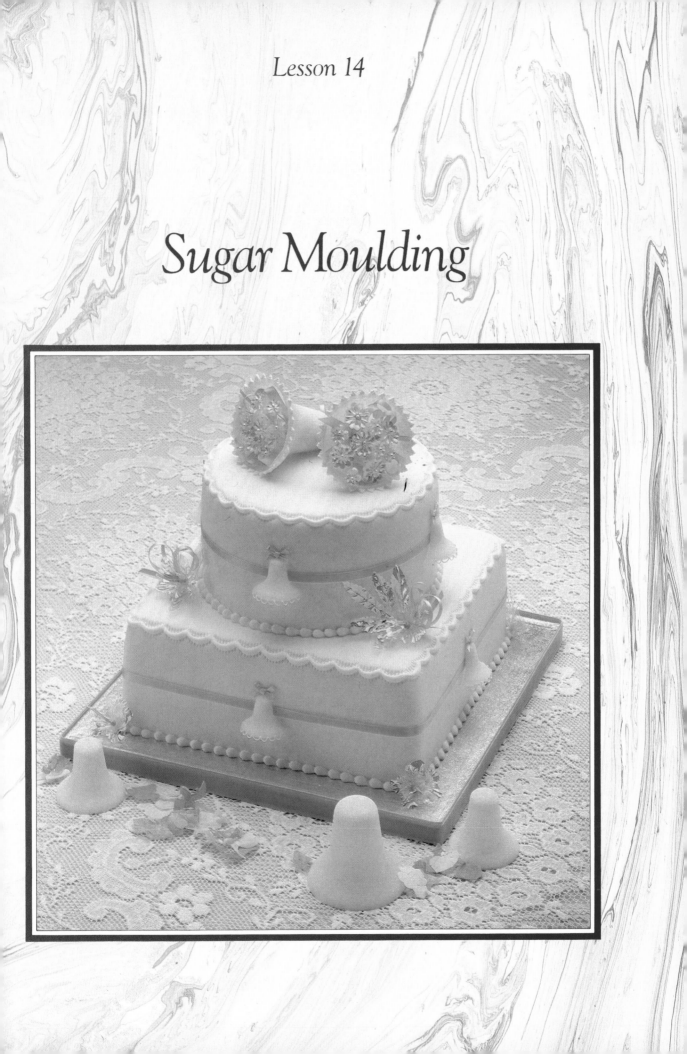

Sugar Moulding

Sugar moulding is a very enjoyable part of cake decoration – it is very easy and someone with no experience in cake decoration can produce very attractive pieces.

The principle is no different from a child filling a bucket at the seaside with damp sand then turning it out to produce the shape of the bucket. For sugar moulding the two ingredients are water and caster (superfine) sugar. A teaspoon, small spatula, cranked palette knife, food colouring and waxed paper will also be needed.

INGREDIENTS
450g (1lb) caster (superfine) sugar
20-30ml (4-6 teaspoons) cold water

If making coloured objects, add food colour to the water before mixing with the sugar.

Place the sugar into a bowl and slowly add the water. Mix through with a spatula. When all the water has been added the mixture should be the consistency of damp sand. Keep the sugar mixture covered with a damp cloth to stop it crusting in the bowl.

Have clean, dry moulds ready. For solid items, pack the mould with sugar using a teaspoon. After two or three teaspoonsful have been put in, pack sugar tightly with the back of a spoon to ensure no gaps or cavities will appear on the finished item. Spoon in more sugar and continue until the mould is full. Using the cranked palette knife, run over the surface of the mould to remove excess sugar and make a level base.

Take a piece of waxed paper slightly larger than the mould. Place over base and carefully flip over holding both waxed paper and mould.

Place on a flat surface to dry. Gently tap the mould and lift. The sugar shape should come away from the mould. If it does not, tap until it comes free. Leave a day to dry out completely before decorating or sticking together.

For hollow objects, fill as for solid objects and turn out on waxed paper. Leave them to form a crust on the surface, then place back into the mould. Use a spoon to remove the damp sugar from the centre, leaving a crystallized translucent shell. The length of time that the shape has to be left before scooping out depends on the size of the piece and the temperature of the room. Once dried the point of a sharp knife should not be able to penetrate into the hard surface.

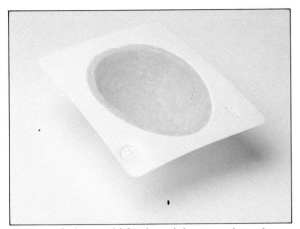

1. Pack the mould firmly with lemon-coloured sugar and use a palette knife to level the base.

2. Turn the mould out onto a piece of waxed paper and set aside until a crust of dried sugar has formed on the surface.

3. Return the egg to the mould and scoop out the damp sugar in the centre of the egg. Turn the egg out of the mould once more and leave until completely dry. Make 2.

4. When dry, trim the rims of the egg shells with a piped garland using a No 6 tube. Decorate the top of the egg with purchased silk flowers and leaves.

5. Stick the base of the second egg shell onto a cake board and trim with a frill. When completely dry, fill with chocolates.

6. When completely dry the egg can be assembled.

Easter Egg

This hollow standard sized egg was moulded in lemon sugar. Fill with mini chocolate eggs, then stick the halves together. Finish with purchased sugar flowers. Pipe a green shell edge with a No1 tube.

Panorama Egg

Mould a hollow lemon egg. Cut off half of one part using a piece of thin wire. Place a piece of waxed paper over cut end so it does not dry out. Leave to form a hard, thin shell, then scoop out the damp sugar remaining in the centre. The bottom half has a small fabric chick placed in it, with some piped grass and mauve forget-me-nots. Stick the lid in position with a little lemon royal icing, pipe a small shell around the side and over the cut edge. Finish with tiny piped flowers in the corners.

Any type of scene can be put into a panorama egg and they can be made in different sizes using the egg moulds available.

Mini Eggs

These solid sugar eggs would be ideal to fill a larger egg. To serve as after dinner mints, add oil of peppermint to the sugar before filling the moulds. Once moulded, turn out and stick the two halves together with a little royal icing. Decoration has been piped on in various colours using No1 tubes.

Sugar Bells

1. Pack a sugar mould tightly with white sugar, turn out and set aside until a crust of dried sugar has formed on the surface.

2. Hollow-out the centre of the bell.

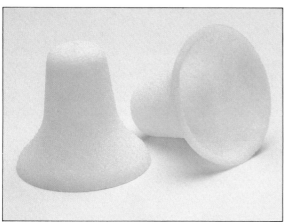

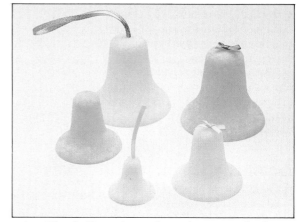

3. Continue to hollow-out the centre until only a thin shell remains.

4. The shells can be made in white sugar, food colouring may be added to the water to create coloured sugar bells.

Holly Plaque

Mould sugar holly leaves and the bell. Leave to dry. Pipe a 15cm (6in) circle onto a plaque or directly onto the cake surface. Using a No1 tube in a bag filled with green royal icing, pipe some spruce and stick the sugar holly in position. Once dry, outline the holly leaves with royal icing. Placing a double figure-of-eight bow at the top of the wreath. Paint the bell with gold food colouring, stick on to the wreath and position a gold stamen into the bell to represent the clanger. Pipe red berries with No1 tube.

Posy Bowls

Mould, dry and hollow out posy bowls, using commercial moulds. These are suitable for use at a dinner party to serve after-dinner mints or chocolates, sugar cubes. If wished, make them in colours to match the table setting. For weddings sugared almonds could be put into these sugar bowls and for children's parties fill with sweets (candies).

Sugar Cubes

Sugar cubes in pretty shapes look festive for a special tea or dinner party. The sugar can be coloured or designs can be piped or stencilled on the surface.

Shell

Mould two halves of a shell using a chocolate mould or a clean scallop shell. Leave to dry slightly and scoop out. Dry. Fill in one half with ribbon loops and flowers. Here silk flowers have been used, but sugar ones could have been chosen. Pipe a line of icing along the back and stick the top half in position. If necessary, support the lid open until the icing dries.

Pink Heart Box

This heart box was made using a chocolate mould. Pack pale pink sugar into the base and lid. Turn out and leave until surface is dry. Scoop out damp sugar and leave pieces to dry completely. The lid has some stems and leaves piped with a No2 tube with green royal icing. Position blossoms with pink royal icing stamens.

Snowman

Mould two halves of a snowman using a chocolate mould. When dry stick the two halves together with royal icing. Plait (braid) some red cord for a scarf or use red marzipan or sugarpaste. Pipe eyes, nose and mouth in black royal icing with a No1 piping tube.

Sugar Mice

These sugar mice are moulded in a commercial mould. While in mould, push in a piece of string for the tail. Turn out and dry. For a child's party sugar mice can be made in a variety of different colours.

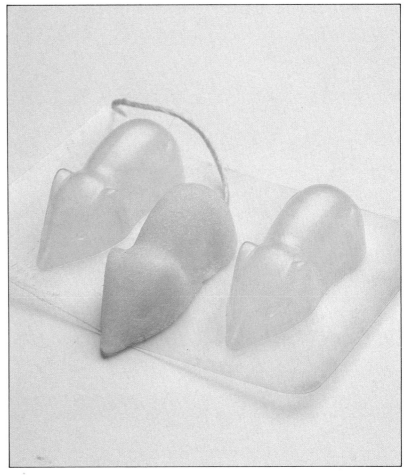

157

Spring Chocolate Box

This brown chocolate box was moulded in a plastic corsage box. Fill the mould in usual way, and hollow out both pieces. Leave to dry. On the top half pipe some stems and leaves and place silk flowers onto the stems. Pipe a dropped line around both sides with dots above. A suitable inscription could be written on the box if desired.

After-Dinner Mints

The after-dinner mints shown here have been moulded in chocolate moulds. Add oil of peppermint to the sugar mixture before packing in the moulds. Once moulded and dried pipe on designs using royal icing. Here a small petal nozzle and No2 tube have been used to make various flowers and patterns.

Frills and Flounces

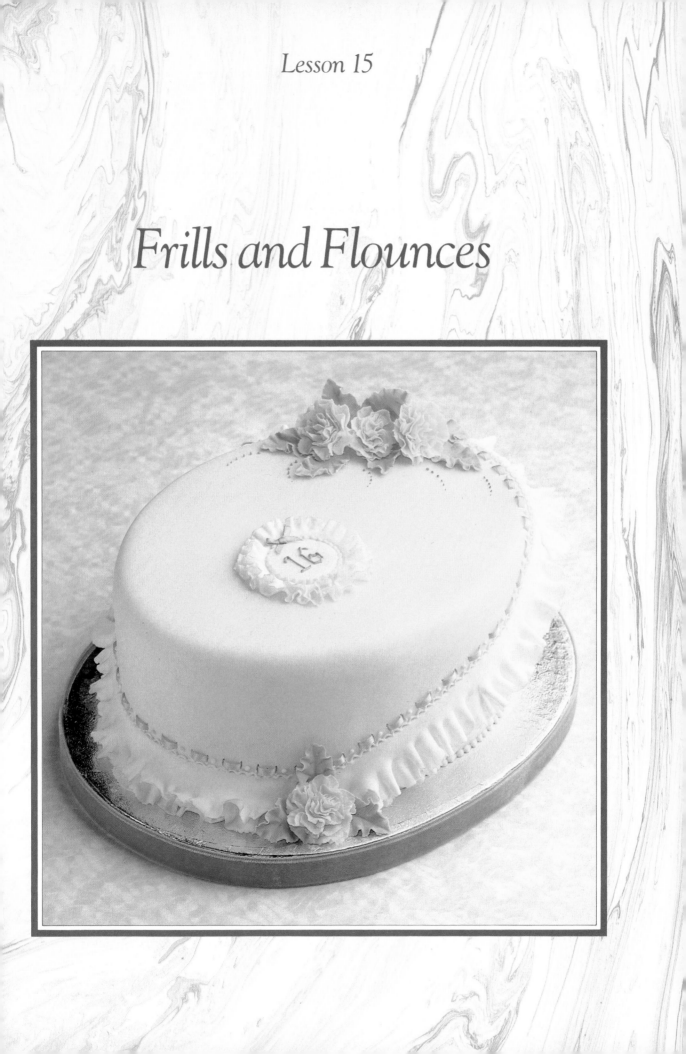

Frills and Flounces

Frills and flounces, which are made in the same way, add pretty, side decorations to sugarpasted or royal iced cakes. Frills can be wide or narrow, white or coloured, single or layered, and in many different combinations.

To make frills or flounces, all that is needed is a cutter, a sharp knife, nonstick worksurface, rolling pin, and cocktail sticks. The most popular frill cutter is the Garrett frill, named after cake decorator Elaine Garrett, who introduced the idea. However, any round cutter, whether fluted or straight, can be used.

To make a frill, roll out sugarpaste until it is almost translucent. Plain sugar can be used, but the frills will hold their shape better if gum tragacanth is added in the proportion of 5ml (1 teaspoon) to 250g (8oz) sugarpaste. Cut out the shape using a cutter. Cut the circle, then gently frill with a cocktail stick, taking care not to stretch or tear the paste. Attach to a sugarpasted cake with a little egg white or water, or by crimping if the coating is fresh. Attach to a royal-iced cake with a thin line of icing.

Frills and flounces can also be used to decorate the top of a cake, on plaques, and to add clothes to modelled figures. Frills and flounces can also be used to make simple flowers, such as carnations.

Small Flower Plaque

This little plaque made from a Garrett frill cutter would be suitable for any type of cake. A small runout, painting or spray of flowers could be put on the plaque with an inscription. If you feel unhappy about writing straight on to the cake surface writing on a plaque is safer, if you do make a mistake you can always make another plaque, but a drastic mistake on to a cake can result in taking off all the icing and re-coating it.

Garrett Frill

Roll out some sugarpaste, cut out with a Garrett frill cutter without the fixed centre. Use a cocktail stick to frill the edge; dry. This plaque was painted with a simple freehand design using food colours. The edge was also dusted with petal dust to give a contrast to the cake surface.

Garrett Frill

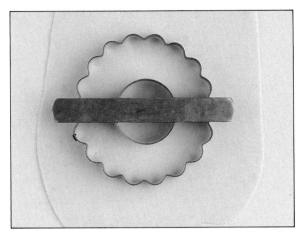

1. Roll out the sugar paste on a lightly cornfloured (cornstarched) surface until it is almost translucent. Cut the shape using a Garrett frill or serrated cutter and the hole using a smaller plain cutter if you are not using a set centre frill cutter. Take care to centre the hole.

2. Carefully frilling the edges of the circle using a cocktail stick by rolling the cocktail stick along the edge of the paste moving all the time to stop it from sticking.

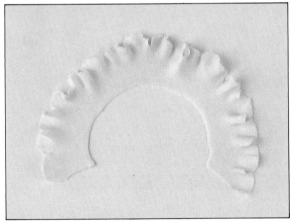

3. Continue frilling the edges all the way around the shape. Cut the ring open with a sharp knife.

4. The frill may then be gently eased open and is ready to be attached to the cake.

Plain Frill

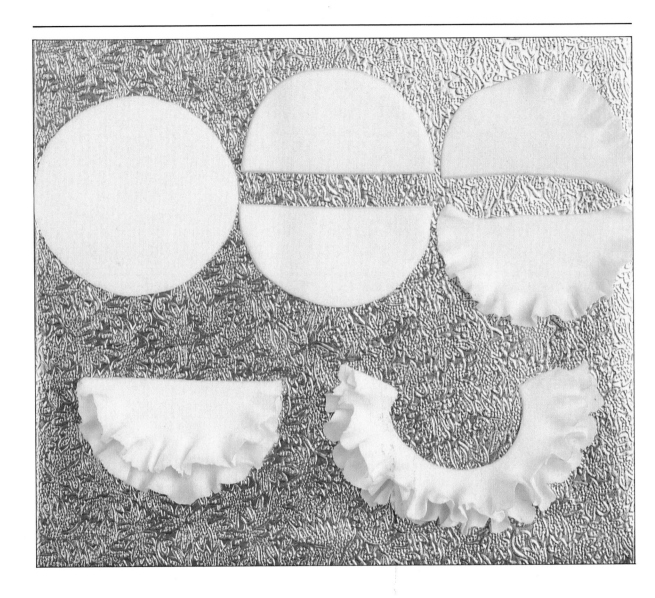

1. Roll out some paste, and cut out using a plain pastry cutter.

2. Cut the circle in half.

3. Frill each half, carefully using a cocktail stick.

4. Lay one half on top of each other, as for a scalloped frill, sticking together with a little egg white. When dry dust the edge with petal dust.

Attaching the Frill

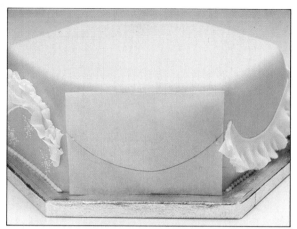

1. Make a paper template to indicate the curve of the frill, attach to the cake securely with pins.

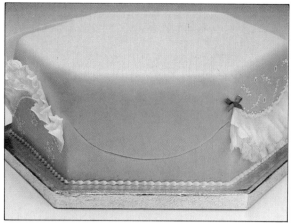

2. Using a scriber or needle scribe the curve-line on the cake.

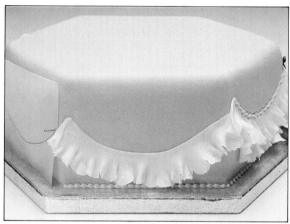

3. Attach the frill to the cake using a little egg-white or water.

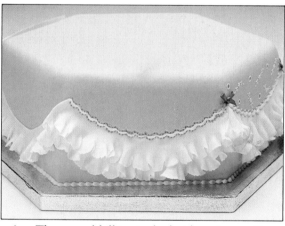

4. The second frill is attached with a crimper. Pipe tiny dots in contrasting colour following the crimped line.

5. Allow to dry thoroughly then dust the edge of the frill with petal dust.

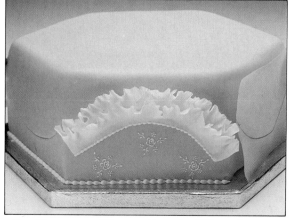

6. To create a different effect, the frill may be attached with the curve in the opposite direction.

Cutout Frills

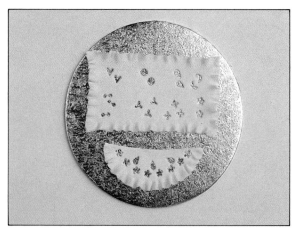

1. Make plaques as described above and press-out the shapes from the paste before crimping.

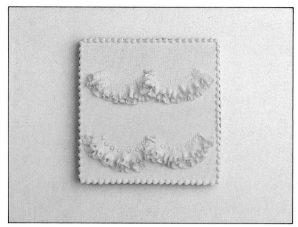

2. If the cutouts are to be on the frilled edges, the shapes should be cut from the paste before the circle is frilled.

Layered Frills

Scalloped frills may be attached in several layers to achieve a variety of different effects.

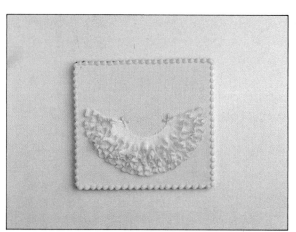

1. Four layers of frill are shown, each dusted with petal dust and finished with piped royal icing.

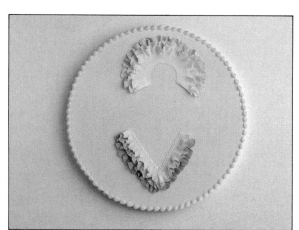

2. The paste is coloured with various amounts of colouring to achieve a graduated effect. The graduated effect is offset by a contrasting frill. The frill is shaped into a 'v' as an alternative to the curve.

Straight Frills

This plaque shows straight frills as an alternative to
scalloped frills

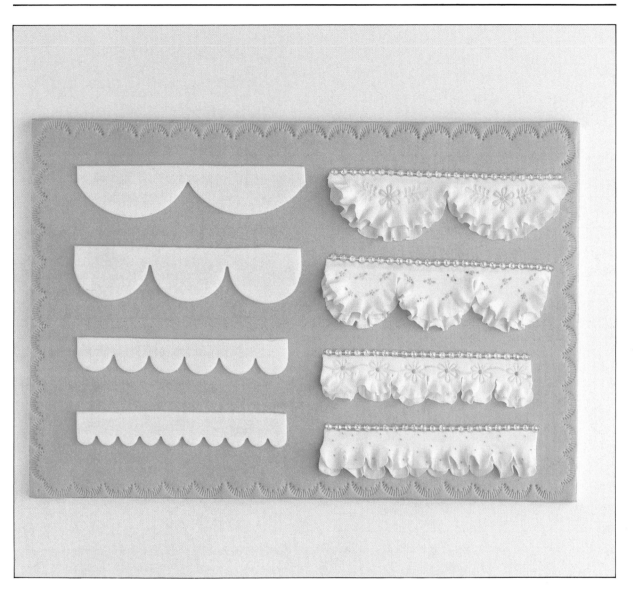

1. This shows a double frill. The top layer is
embossed with a daisy and leaf design. When dry,
dust the bottom edge. Pearls have been placed on the
top edge.

2. The frill shown here has forget-me-nots and
leaves painted with food colouring. Once dry dust
the edge.

3. Another double-layered frill with embossed
daisies along its length. Paint in the stems and
centres of the daisies.

4. This narrow double frill has tiny piped dots all
over the surface.

Pastry Cutter Carnation

These quick little carnations are made with sugarpaste. They can be made white and dusted with petal dust or, as shown, in a pastel shade and then dusted with additional petal dust to give a natural effect.

The carnation sizes can be altered by using different sized cutters: the smaller the cutter the smaller the finished flower will be. In damp or humid conditions a little gum tragacanth should be kneeded into the paste. Use approximately 2.5ml (½ teaspoon) to 250g (8oz) of paste. Leave half an hour before using. Keep in a polythene bag to prevent it from drying out.

1. Roll out the paste on a lightly cornfloured (corn-starched) surface. Using a serrated pastry cutter cut out the shape. The paste should be thin to ensure good frilling.

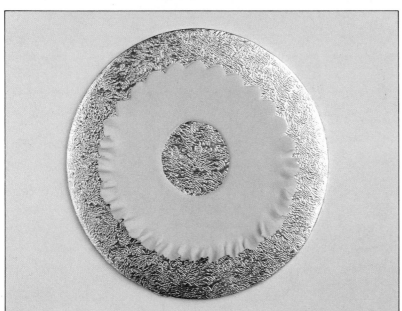

2. Cut a hole in the centre using a small round cutter. Using a cocktail stick dipped in a little cornflour, start frilling the edges only.

3. Continue frilling the edges all the way around, then cut open the ring with a sharp knife.

4. Gently use your fingers to pleat the straight side and shape into a straight edge. Do not worry if bottom cracks, as it will be trimmed off afterwards.

5. Brush some egg white along the strip from the bottom to where the frill starts. Starting at the left-hand end, roll up. The first 5cm (2in) should be rolled tightly to ensure a good centre and overall shape.

6. Continue rolling, making sure the overlap is stuck round, then use scissors to cut off the excess paste. Place the carnation into a small artist's pallet until it is dry.

Frilled Leaves

1. Colour some sugarpaste green. Roll out thinly on a lightly cornfloured (corn-starched) surface.

2. Using a cocktail cutter or a cardboard template, cut out the leaf shape.

3. Using a cocktail stick start frilling the edge.

4. Continue frilling all the way around the edge of the leaf.

5. Place on a piece of foam rubber. Mark the veins on the leaf with a cocktail stick.

6. To finish off the leaf mark the central vein and leave to dry. The leaves can be placed over formers or crumpled up tissue so they dry in a natural, individual form.

Frilled Plaques

1. Cut out some white paste using two sizes of plain pastry cutters. Completely frill both circles.

2. Brush a little egg white into the centre of the large round. Stick the smaller one on top of the larger one. Using the thicker end of the pastry cutter mark a ring as a guideline to pipe around. Dry for 2 to 3 hours.

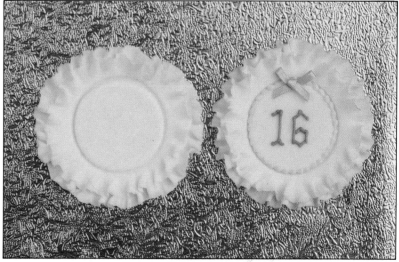

3. Brush a little petal dust on the edge. Match the frill, if using on a cake. Using lemon icing and a No1 tube, pipe a small shell around the marked circle. Pipe '16', or another inscription. Finish off with a miniature bowl.

Sweet Sixteen Cake

Marzipan a 20cm (8in) oval fruit cake. Cover with lemon sugarpaste and transfer onto a 25cm (10in) oval board. Dry for 2 days.

Using a scriber or needle, scribe a line onto the cake surface. This makes attaching a frill easier as you have a guideline to follow for keeping a straight line. Start the line two-thirds of the way along on the left-hand side, bring the line up at a fairly steep angle, go along the top edge, down the other side and round to meet at the board. Pipe a lemon shell around the base using a No2 tube. Attach a white double frill. Pipe a scalloped line above it with a No1 tube, then put a line of narrow ribbon insertion above the frill. Pipe a dot of icing in between each piece of ribbon.

Make ten leaves and four carnations. Place three leaves and one carnation for the bottom spray, sticking in position with royal icing. The top spray is assembled out of seven leaves and three carnations.

Make a frilled plaque and position.

Dust the frill around the cake. This should always be dry before you dust it as if it is soft you will squash it. A violet/mauve petal dust was used with a little additional lilac lustre colour to give a slight sheen. Using a number three or four brush that should be dry, dust the frill from the outside to get a density of colour on the edge of frills.

Additional designs suitable for use on frilled plaques.

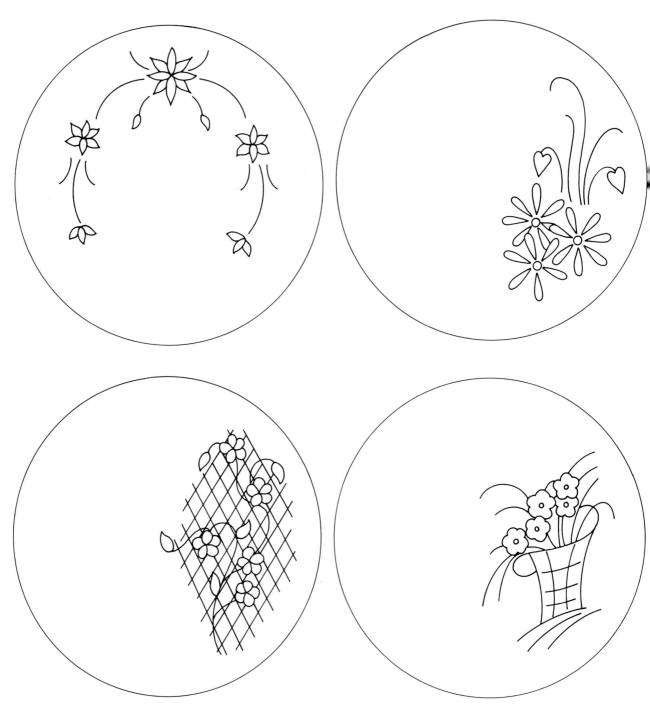

Lesson 16

Runout Borders and Collars

Runout Collars

Runout work is an important feature of royal icing. It is very popular in competition work because of the intricate designs that can be achieved. There are two main types of runout collars, simple collars and sectional collars.

The sectional pieces do not have to be designed each time, as you design them once to fit say a 20cm (8in) square then each time you coat a 20cm (8in) square cake these pieces will fit. Each full collar must be individually designed because every time you marzipan and ice a cake it will vary slightly in size. You have to be a little bit of a mathematician as well as a cake decorator to draw the collars to fit accurately.

In addition to your normal cake decorating you will need drawing paper, compass set, pencil, ruler, fine paintbrushes and a good quality waxed paper.

Icing
Icing made with pure albumum powder is the best type of icing to use for runout collars as boosted albumum substitute is not really strong enough. Softening the icing as necessary by

adding cold water a little at a time to the piping consistency of royal icing. Leave to stand for at least an hour before using to enable the icing to settle and the air bubbles to surface.

Unfortunately there is no hard and fast rule as to how much water to add to the royal icing because different consistencies are used for different types of runout. As a general guideline, lift a little icing up on a spoon and let it run back into the

172

bowl, its trail should disappear on a count of 8 to 10. If the trail does not disappear, add some more water to the icing. If the trail disappears after 3 or 4 seconds, add some more royal icing. After doing a few runout collars and borders you will get to know the correct consistency for each individual collar.

Attaching Collars
When the collars are dry, remove from the waxed paper using a fine cranked palette knife. Another method is to bring the collar to the edge of the table top and pull the waxed paper down at right angles, carefully going around until the collar is removed. Pipe a line with a No2 tube in the same colour as the base icing and put the collar on the cake, making sure it is evenly positioned.

Borders
There are three ways of attaching a collar or border, to the cake board. The first is to make the border and let it dry, then slide it over the top and down the side of the cake. However, if the sides are not perfectly straight or if the board coating is slightly uneven the collar may break. The easiest method is to do a runout directly on to the board using a pattern. Make a single cut in the paper pattern, open it up and place it around the cake. Join the cut ends and pipe a line slightly outside the template; allow to dry for a few minutes, then remove the pattern. Flood the area from the line to the edge of the cake with icing. Alternatively, pipe a freehand line on the board and then flood.

The final method has to be done in a fairly dark room. Place a desk lamp about 30cm (12in) above the cake and shine onto the centre. This has to be done after the top collar has been positioned. The collar will cast a shadow on the cake board and all you have to do is to pipe a line along the edge of the shadow on the board.

Making a Collar

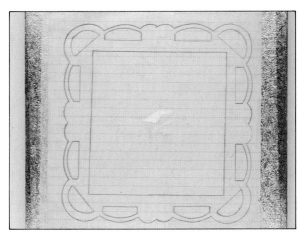

1. Measure the top of the cake and draw a template of the collar design on a piece of paper. Attach securely to a glass or board surface. Secure a piece of waxed paper over the design.

2. Pipe a line of royal icing over the pencil lines on the template.

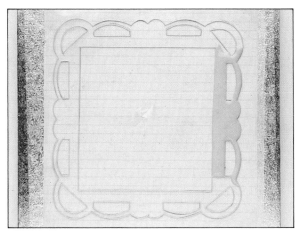

3. Flood the collar section by section working quickly but neatly.

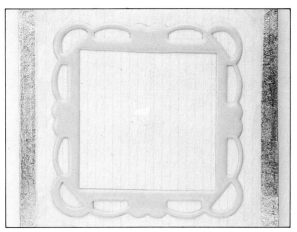

4. Continue flooding until the collar is completely filled. Dry thoroughly overnight.

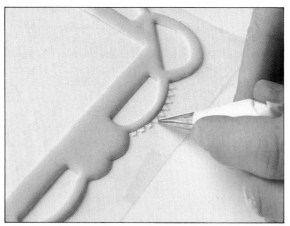

5. Pipe petit point around the outer edge of the dried collar.

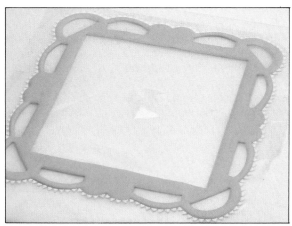

6. Continue piping until the collar is completed. Dry thoroughly.

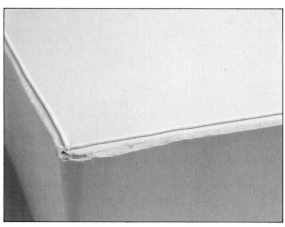

7. Pipe a solid line of icing around the top of the cake upon which to fix the collar.

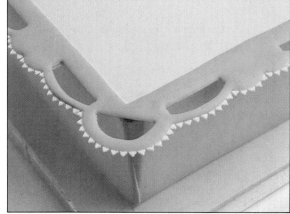

8. Remove the collar carefully from the waxed paper using a fine cranked palatte knife. Position the collar on the cake.

Pink Collar

When the runout icing on this collar is quite dry, dry pipe some stems and leaves with a No0 tube and then attach some blossom made with an ejector. Just before cutting the blossom, pipe a small dot of icing to mark where each one will go. Once positioned pipe a small dot of pink icing in the centre of each flower to represent the stamen. Pipe the edging using a No0 tube.

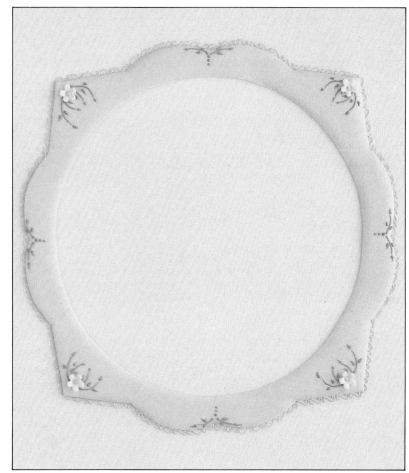

White Holly Collar

This solid white collar has holly leaf embroidery piped all over the surface usng a No00 tube and green icing. Use red icing and No0 tube to pipe the berries. A half-diamond edging is piped using the No0 red tube, pipe small dots on the points.

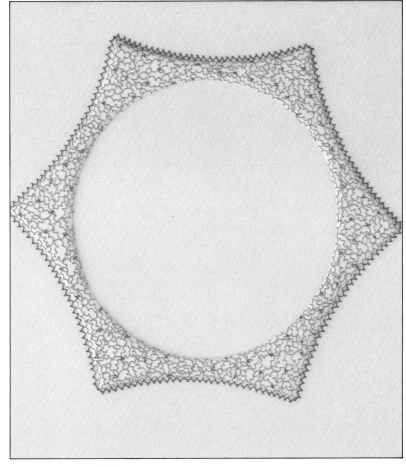

Collar Sections

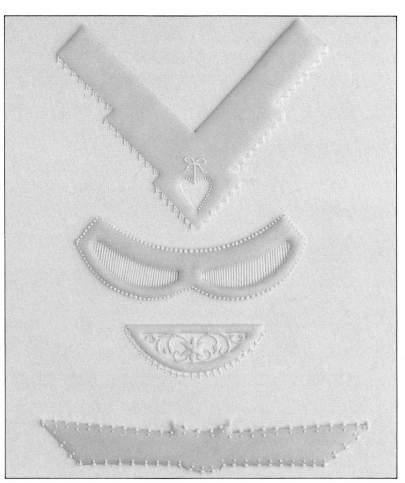

A pink corner section suitable for a square cake. Pipe 3:2:1 petit point lace edging with No0 tube and a dot beading around the heart.

Dry the lilac sectional runout, then turn over and pipe fine lines with No0 tube across the two gaps. Let these dry and turn the collar over. Pipe beading around the edge.

A small pink sectional runout with flowers and stems piped with a No1 tube before the edge is flooded.

A plain lilac runout section suitable for the top edge of a square cake. Pipe a scalloped rope with a No1 tube.

This sectional collar was made in lilac royal icing. The S and C scroll pattern has been piped using a No1 tube.

This corner section is suitable for a square cake. The solid band of lemon runout is then filigree piped using a No1 tube. The outer line has been piped using green royal icing and a No0 tube.

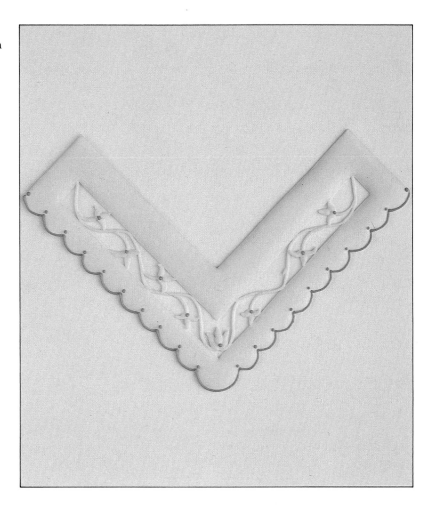

The lilac sectional collar was decorated with a daisy and leaf design piped with a No1 tube.

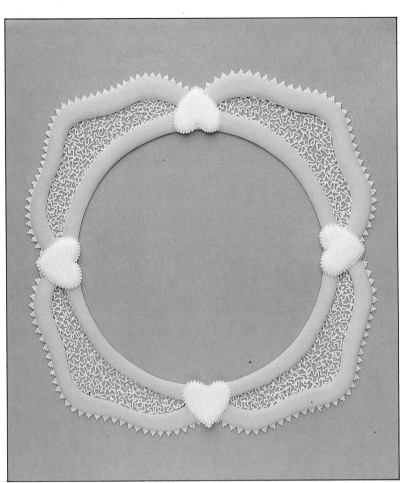

Open Collar with Hearts

Make a plain runout collar from the template and four hearts. The collar shown here is in lemon and the hearts in white. Once the collar is dry, pipe cornelli work in the four sections with a No0 tube. Pipe a beaded edging on the hearts. When dry, remove from the waxed paper and stick on the collars with small dots of royal icing. Pipe 3:2:1 edging around the edge of the collar.

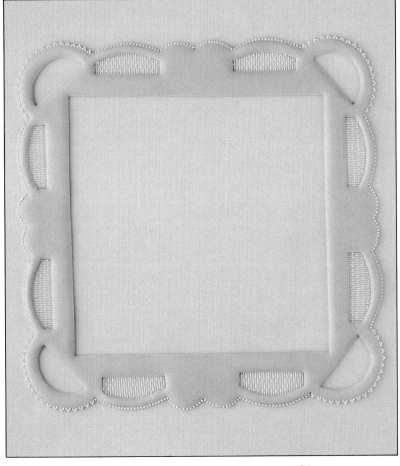

Lilac Collar

This collar with dainty line work has been flooded in lilac. When dry, pipe lines with a No0 tube. Allow to dry, turn over and pipe tiny dots on the lines, alternating the dots to give an attractive finish. Pipe pearly edging along the sides and finish with 2:1 petit point lace.

Lemon Collar

This yellow hexagonal collar has a flower and leaf cutout. The collar inside line was piped, then the flower and leaf design. Once dry, pipe scalloped line with a No0 tube, then pipe a small shell from the centre of the scallop outwards. The plaque has some fine lines piped on to show how to finish off the inside edge.

Peach Collar

This solid peach runout, has white cornelli work piped all over it using a No0 tube. Add petit point 3:2:1 lace around the edge in a darker shade of peach.

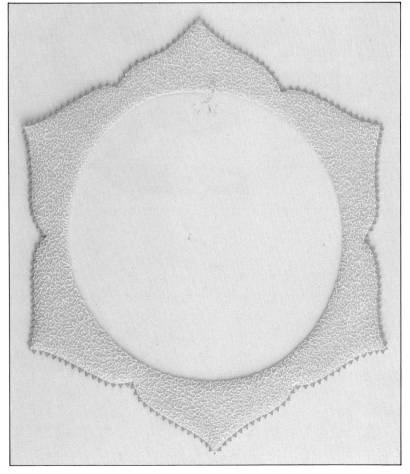

179

These two sectional runout pieces are suitable for use on a circular or oval cake. The edging has been worked in peach royal icing using a No0 tube.

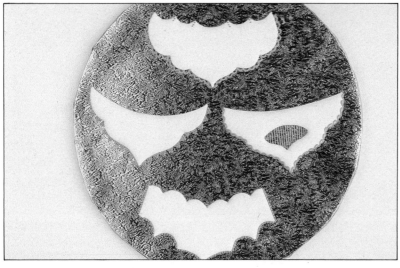

Three solid sectional pieces and one with cutout trellis work. The edging has been worked in peach using a No0 tube.

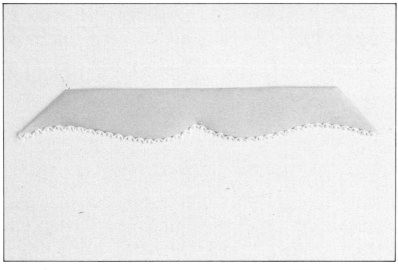

This solid pink sectional runout was designed to sit along the edge of a square cake. The piped edging was worked in white using a No0 tube.

Christmas Collar

This collar sits on the top surface of the cake, instead of on the edge. This type of collar would be suitable if you were not satisfied with the coating on your cake, as it would cover up any imperfections. All the decoration is in the collar, the only thing that is added is the inscription. Flood the collar in white, then dry for 30 minutes. Flood the candle with red. Leave to dry, then flood in a mixture of orange and red runout for the flame, followed by softened red for the wax. The holly is outlined and then flooded in green; dry, then add red berries. Pipe edging using a paper piping-bag with 'v' cut for the leaf shape. Pipe small leaves around the edge, then pipe on the red berries using a No1 tube. Dry for 24 hours.

181

Templates for runout collars and
sections. These may be sized up or
down to fit the required cake.

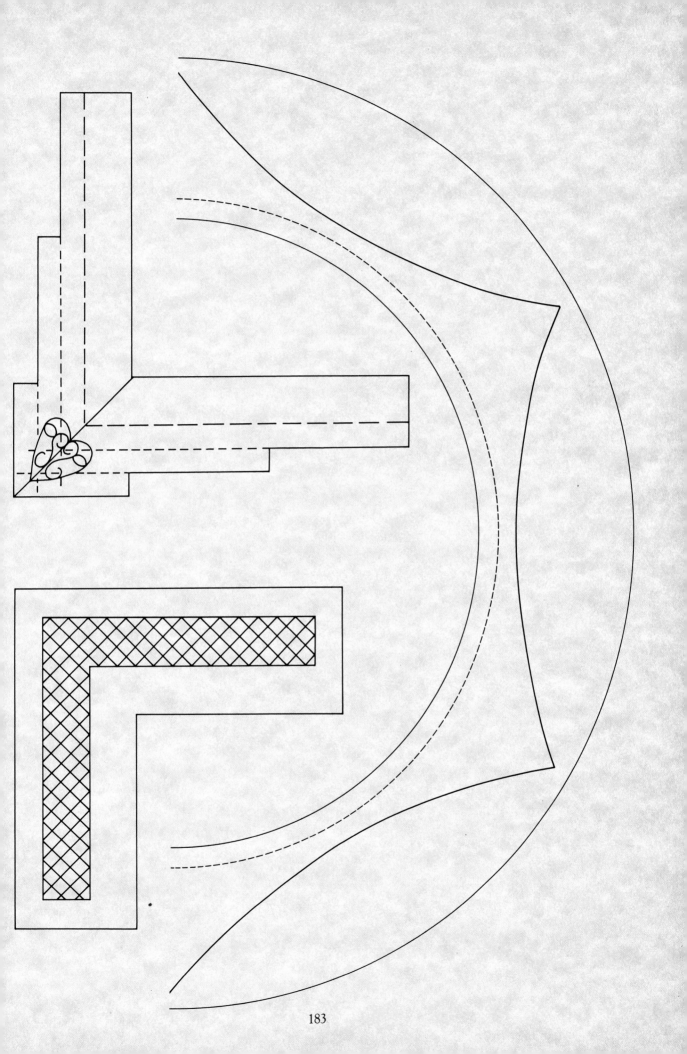

Templates for runout collars and sections.

Piped Top and Side Designs

Piped Top and Side Designs

The top and side designs piped on a cake can be as simple or as elaborate as your time and skill allow. Sugarpasted, royal-iced and buttercreamed cakes can all be decorated in this way, although it is best to stick to simple designs if working in buttercream.

Ideas for piped top and side designs can be found everywhere. Use the designs in this book, picture books, greetings cards, pattern books, magazines, etc. A nice idea for a child's birthday cake is to copy one of the child's own drawings in icing.

An experienced cake decorator should be able to pipe the designs on a cake freehand. If you are not confident enough to do this, trace the design and lightly scribe it onto the cake. When tracing side designs,

allow for any curves in a round, oval or heart-shaped cake. Remember to size up or size down the basic design if piping on a tiered wedding cake.

For accuracy when piping elaborate or geometric designs, plan the work on graph paper first, then transfer to the cake top and sides. For all designs, have all the bags of coloured icing fitted with tubes before you begin, so that you can work quickly. It is not always necessary to dry one colour before piping the next, particularly

when working in royal icing.

Pipe top designs with the cake flat, as though you were painting or drawing on paper. For the side designs, you may find it easier to tilt the cake, either on a tilting turntable or by placing something under it while you work.

Practice the design on a cake board or on the worksurface before piping on the cake. Mistakes can not always be rectified, as coloured icing will stain the cake surface.

The only necessary equipment is a number of paper piping bags and an assortment of tubes. For more elaborate designs, tracing paper, pencil, scribe and graph paper will be useful.

Halloween Plaque

This simple design would be suitable for a Halloween Cake. Scribe the pattern on the plaque from the template. Fill a small bag fitted with a No1 tube with black royal icing and pipe the witch, but not the hand and face profile. Pipe the 'Halloween' inscription freehand in black. The face and hand are piped in white and the moon in yellow. The bats are also piped freehand. Pipe a white edging with a No42 tube, then pipe a yellow and black scalloped line inside the outer shell.

Bird Table Plaque

This white plaque shows a design which may be piped freehand or by copying the template. All the work has been piped using a No1 tube. The bird table is brown, the grass, stems and leaves in green and the flowers in mauve and blue. The pulled shell has been piped with a No7 tube.

Butterfly Plaque

This wedgwood blue plaque shows a design suitable for a small cake. With the exception of the butterfly, it is all worked freehand, although you could scribe some guidelines on to the cake. The stems, leaves, flowers and words were all piped with a No1 tube. Pipe the butterfly wings with a No0 tube, and dry flat on waxed paper. Once dry, pipe a body using a No1 tube, directly onto the cake surface, stick the wings into position and support until dry with two pieces of folded paper or foam. Two stamens are used for the antenna. This design could be piped in any colour combination. Pipe the edging in a herringbone pattern with a No2 tube.

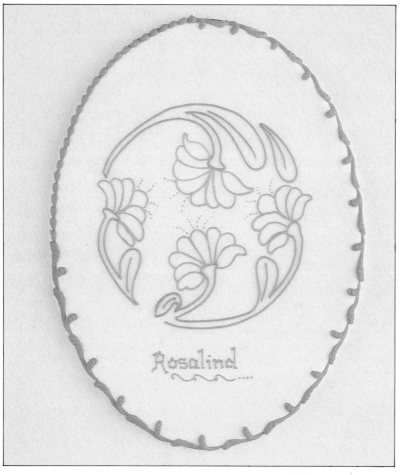

Oval Plaque

This simple line work design has pink flowers and green leaves, both piped with a No1 tube. The inscription in the same shade of pink is worked with a No0 tube. The edging features a quarter section of shells and three-quarter small S and C scrolls piped with a No2 tube.

Plaque with Silk Flowers

This quick and effective decoration is suitable for a single tier celebration cake. A spray of yellow silk flowers and ribbon loops has been used, but sugar flowers could be used in place of the silk ones. Five figure-of-eight bows were used, made and arranged with the flowers using a small piece of sugarpaste to secure. Pipe a little embroidery using a No0 tube. A suitable inscription can be piped on the plaque. Pipe the edge with a No42 tube in a scalloped rope design. A smaller No1 scalloped rope line sits inside the boarder edging.

Swan Plaque

This square design is made with a paper template. Cut a circle of greaseproof (waxed) paper, and fold into eight equal sections. Draw on one segment, and then fold up and cut to make the pattern. Place the pattern on the plaque and scribe a line along the edge. Remove the pattern and pipe a small shell with a No1 tube; cornelli the outer section with a No0 tube. The centre of the design has forget-me-nots piped all over the surface, leaving a small area for an inscription. The feature decoration is a runout sugar swan with ribbon loops and small pink fabric roses.

Wedgwood Plaque

This Wedgwood blue plaque has a runout waterlily with a pressure-piped cherub in the centre. Pipe the cherub on both sides. A cutout ejector blossom is attached to the cherub's foot. The outer part of the plaque features Wedgwood-style piped embroidery of fruit, vases, wheat, grapes and flowers using a No1 tube.

Oak Leaf Plaque

The plaque shown has a very simple but effective runout design. Make a pattern from the template, scribe on the surface and outline the leaves in green with a No1 tube. Using runout icing in the same shade, flood in the leaves. The acorns are done in the same way, using brown icing. An inscription can be piped in the centre. Pipe the edge with a No5 tube in a running scroll pattern.

Honeysuckle Plaque

The use of stencils in combination with piping and runouts is shown here. Place the honeysuckle stencil on the plaque surface. Mix white and yellow icing on the table and spread a little over the back of the stencil. By using white and yellow mixed you will get a more natural effect. Pipe the stems directly on the plaque, outline the leaf shapes and flood with some softened icing. Pipe a filigree butterfly flat on waxed paper. When dry, carefully remove the wings and stick into a body that has been piped directly on the plaque. Arrange two stamens for antenna. Pipe the pulled shell edge with a No6 tube.
(See photograph on page 185)

Figure 1 Plaque

Draw the outline of the figure 1 on tracing paper. Scribe onto the surface of the plaque or cake. Outline number using a No1 tube and flood. Leave to dry. The rabbit on the swing can be painted free-hand, as shown, or the design can be incorported or made as part of the runout design. The rabbit here was painted in food colouring diluted with clear spirit. The 'today' was piped directly onto the surface. Use a No5 tube for the shell edging.

Small Wedding Cake

Cover a 20cm (8in) round cake with white royal icing and place on a 25cm (10in) board.

Runout one large heart and four smaller hearts, pipe some small doves and bells. When the runouts are dried, pipe a picot edge around each one. Eject a small blossom straight onto the smaller one, sticking on with a little dot of icing. Pipe some stems and leaves and two initials. Here an N and S have been piped with No0 tube. Let the initials dry, then paint with silver. The larger heart has three blossoms in a spray with some leaves. Pipe an inscription with a No0 tube and paint with silver when dry.

Make a greaseproof (waxed) paper circle the size of the top of the cake. Fold in half, and in half again to get quarters, unfold and place on top of the cake. Mark a dot on the cake where each of the four fold lines meet the top edge. Using a No0 tube and a ruler, mark a dot 2.5cm (1in) each side of the centre dot and 2.5cm (1in) in from the centre dot. Scrape off the centre dot and you should be left with three dots, two on the edge and one 2.5cm (1in) from the edge. Repeat to make four groups of three dots.

Using a No1 tube, join the dot 2.5cm (1in) from the edge to the two dots on the edge. Tilt the cake and pipe a dropped line from one to the other. Using the No0 tube, cornelli the inside area. Pipe a scalloped line along the two top sides and around the dropped line. Repeat on the other three sections.

Stick the large heart into the centre of the cake. Stick the small hearts under the cornelli sections and pipe a set of S and C scrolls with reverse S and C scrolls in each of the four areas with a No42 tube. Pipe a shell border with the No42 tube. A pair of tiny flying doves are piped underneath the scrolls. Pipe a dropped line under the scrolls, with a scalloped line below. A pair of miniature bells sit under the point where the two C scrolls meet.

Using lilac icing pipe a dot with a No1 tube in the centre of each of the flowers. Pipe a scalloped rope around the shells.

Pipe the first lines of the trellis on the scrolls with the No1 tube. The first stage are vertical lines piped at an angle starting from the end of the C scroll. Bring across to meet the S scroll. Repeat on both sides of the scrolls and on all four sets. Let dry for 10 minutes.

Pipe the horizontal lines on the scrolls following the shape and then pipe a white roped line with the No1 tube on top. Finish with a miniature bow on each of the points where the C scrolls meet.

Pipe clangers for the bells and pipe some dots down the side of the cake. Finish off by placing a matching ribbon around the board.
(See photograph on page 186)

Templates for the plaques
illustrated in this chapter.

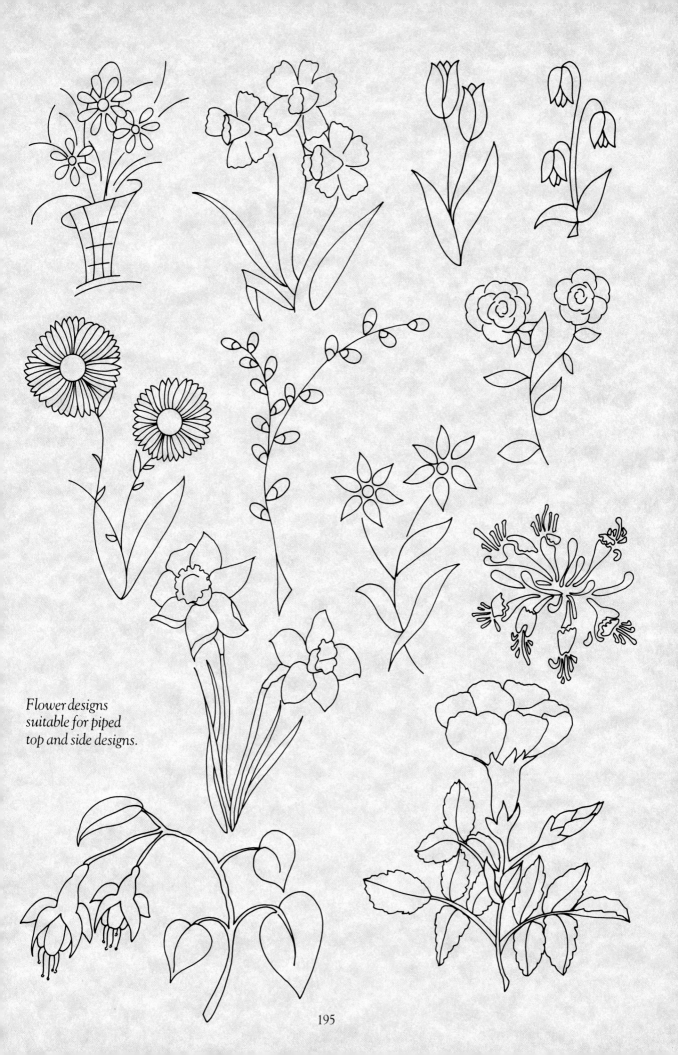

Flower designs suitable for piped top and side designs.

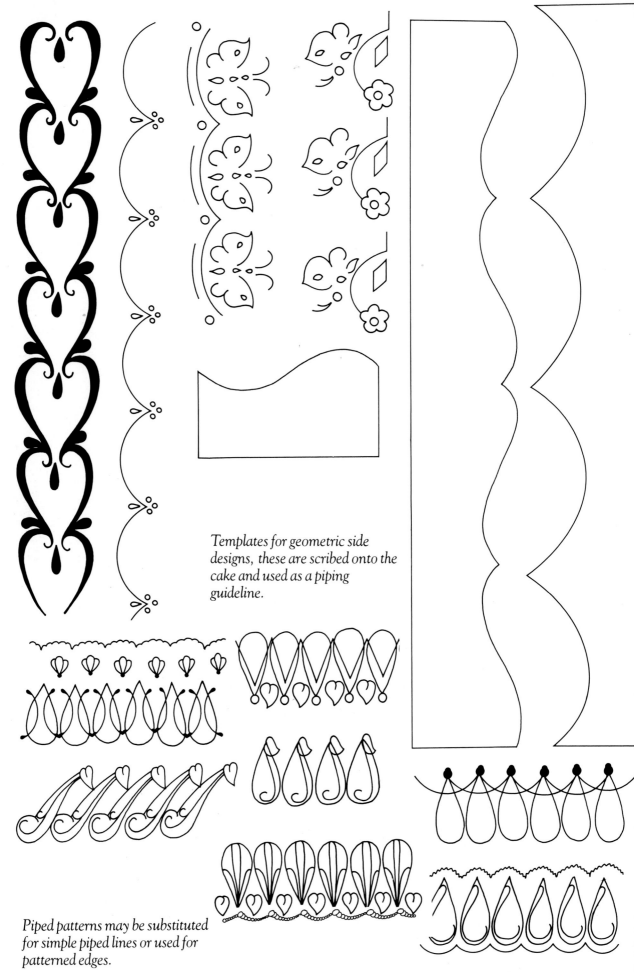

Templates for geometric side designs, these are scribed onto the cake and used as a piping guideline.

Piped patterns may be substituted for simple piped lines or used for patterned edges.

Lettering

Lettering

The most common problem is that many people have not developed a distinctive style. Many types of lettering are shown in this book, but the direct-piped basic lettering on page 214 is a good one to master.

Initially you will have no particular lettering style and although when designing and decorating a cake you will have a pre-conceived idea of what it will look like once decorated and usually it will match your expectations. However, the lettering may be a disappointment because the free-hand lettering style was not well executed. Sometimes it can be too flowing, too curly, going uphill, going downhill and sometimes cramped in areas to small to fit.

It is, therefore, necessary to develop a style of lettering to use for all general work. Once you find one that suits you, study it in depth, draw it out and place in a wipe-clean plastic

Lettering is very important, and if badly executed it can ruin an otherwise attractive cake. People often express a wish to write well on cakes but as with all piping techniques, lettering takes a lot of practice to perfect. If only making one or two inscribed cakes a year, you will not get sufficient experiance to write confidently.

folder. Using a No1 tube, practise going over the shapes of the letters again and again. Try writing a letter in the chosen style; while chatting on the telephone doodle on the telephone pad. All of these things help you to learn the lettering style inside and out, and eventually you will know each letter. With your first few cakes you will need the script for reference, but as you become more experienced you will be able to write freehand.

Start off practising on a piece of glass or board so you can clean off and start again. Start with the common day-to-day inscriptions such as Happy Birthday, Congratulations, Anniversary. Learn to use letter-number association, which sounds complicated but is very easy. Associate letters with a familiar inscription which has the same number of letters. For example Love and Nick both have four letters. Once you have practised basic inscriptions, you will know how much room Love will take, and because Nick will be the same size, you know how much room to allocate on the cake surface. By using letter-number association you will always get perfect spacing and never run out of room.

If the total number of individual letters is less than a basic inscription, you should, with a little experience, realize that a name is one letter shorter than Birthday. Start half-way along the B, if writing directly underneath, so the final letter finishes half-way under the Y.

Once letter-number spacing is mastered, you will never have any problems with spacing or running out of room to pipe an inscription. Similarly consistency with the height of letters also comes with practice.

Freehand lettering is most commonly used on cakes, but runout, pressure-piped, direct-piped runout styles can be used on special cakes.

Freestyle Lettering

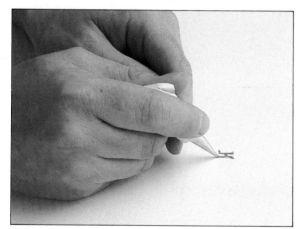

1. Have all your equipment ready before you begin.

2. Place a small amount of icing in the bag and begin writing using firm but even pressure.

3. Take care to get the spacing even and ensure that all the tops and tails are of equal height.

4. Words on the second line should be spaced centrally below the first line.

Runout Lettering 1

This method is worked directly onto
the cake.

1. Trace the letters onto small
pieces of tracing paper.

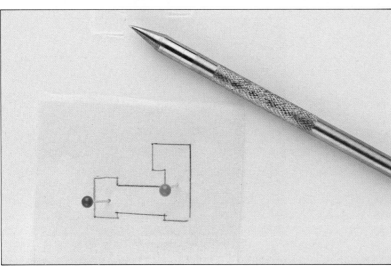

2. Pin the tracings onto the cake
placing the pins in the centre
of the letter which will later be
flooded. Scribe the letter onto the
base icing.

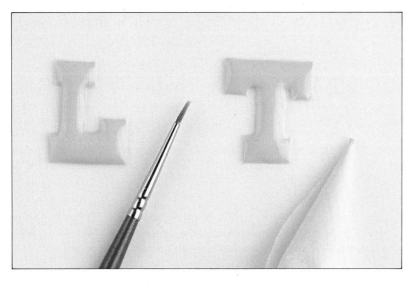

3. Outline the letter using a No1
tube and allow to dry. Flood
and brush smooth and even with a
fine paintbrush.

Runout Lettering 2

This method is worked on waxed paper and then transferred to the cake when dry.

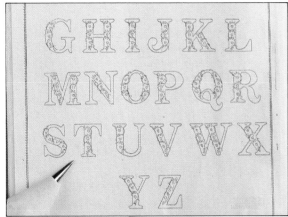

1. Place the chosen lettering in a plastic file. Secure small pieces of waxed paper over the letters to be traced and iced.

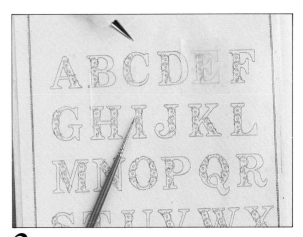

2. Outline the letter using a No1 tube.

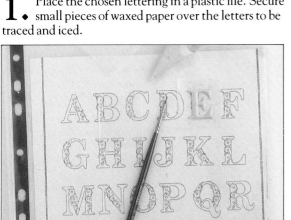

3. Flood the letter brushing it smooth and even with a fine paintbrush.

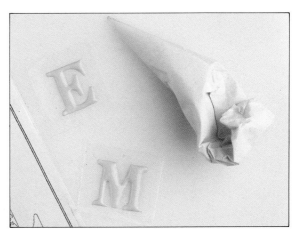

4. The letters should be completely dry before transferring to the cake.

5. Peel the letters off the waxed paper and attach to the cake using small dots of icing.

Monograms

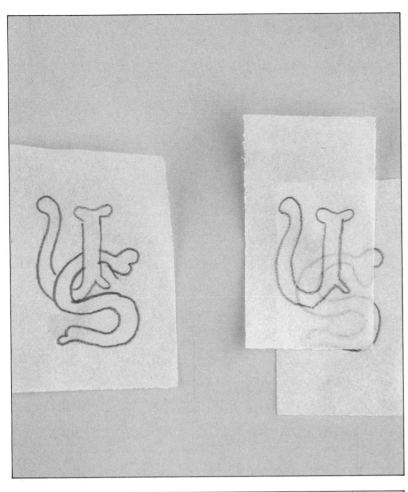

1. The two letters that have to be made into a monogram. Trace each one on a separate piece of tracing or greaseproof paper.

2. Move the letters about until you can overlap them with minimum crossovers. If too much of one letter is covered up, it is hard to read the finished monogram.

3. Once you are happy with the positioning, pin the papers together or place a piece of sticky tape over them to stop them moving.

4. Make a tracing of the completed monogram.

5. Scribe onto the plaque or cake surface using a scriber or hat pin.

6. Outline with ordinary consistency icing using a No0 or 1 tube, depending on the size of the letters – here a No1 was used.

7. The partly completed monogram. The N has been flooded. Let dry for about 30 minutes, then flood the S. It is important to dry one letter first because if you flood both letters at the same time they merge into each other and definition is lost. Monograms can be flooded in the same colours, different colours or shades of the same colour.

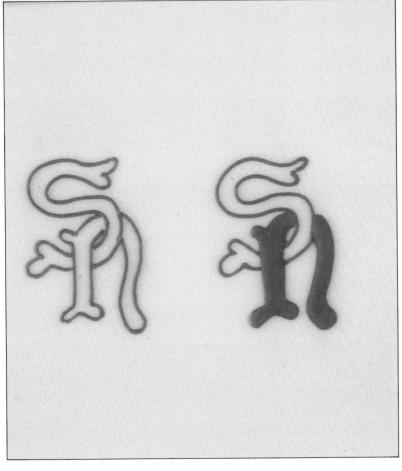

Christmas Plaques

These plaques show different types of script for Christmas cakes, but the styles could be adapted to other suit other types of inscription.

Best Wishes Mother

This simple runout lettering on a square plaque shows how block and decorative lettering styles can be used together. The Best Wishes is a normal block runout lettering style and the Mother is in large runout Old English script, with half of the M in yellow and half in white for contrast.

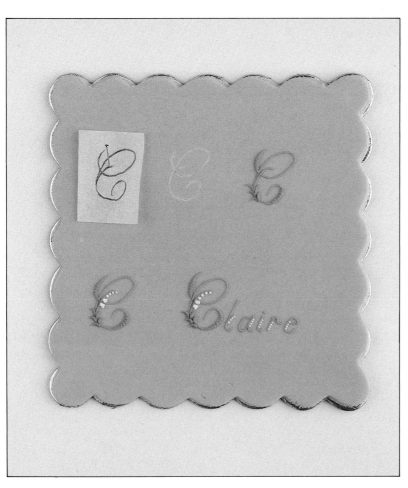

Lily of the Valley Script

The attractive lily of the valley lettering shown is adapted from an embroidery book.

1. Trace the basic line of the letter onto the tracing paper. Do not worry about the finer detail as this is added freehand. This design can be adapted for monograms which look pretty on the side of a wedding cake.

2. Scribe the letter onto the plaque or cake surface.

3. Pipe the basic line in green icing using a No1 piping tube.

4. Working from your pattern, fill in all the fine detail. The flowers are piped in a No0 tube and the leaves in a No1.

5. The finished name Claire with the lace is piped on freehand.

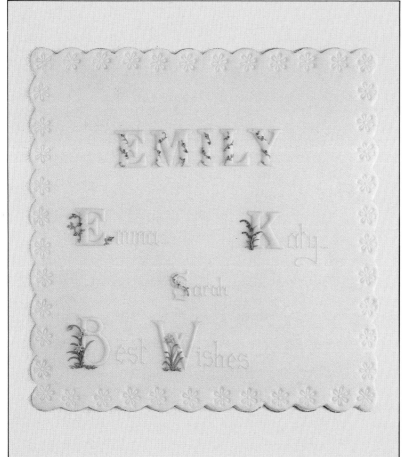

Floral Lettering

The examples show how to use embroidery techniques for lettering. The name Emily is in block runouts from the alphabet given. Pipe each letter required onto waxed paper, dry then stick to the cake surface. Pipe a rambling rose design up the letters, as shown, with a No0 tube with green icing. The rose buds are small shells piped in red, then pipe on tiny calyxes using the green piping tube.

Emma has a flooded first letter and the rest of the name is piped freehand.

Katy and Sarah have been piped the same way as Emma, but have been decorated in slightly different ways.

The Best Wishes has the B and W directly flooded onto the plaque and the rest piped freehand. The letters have been decorated with tiny piped daffodils.

Pressure-piped Gothic Lettering

1. Cover the lettering with plastic. Secure pieces of waxed paper over the letters to be traced.

2. Using a No 1 tube and white icing, pipe over the outline of the letter.

3. Pressure pipe in the denser parts of the letter as you work. Continue until all the letters are copied. Allow to dry.

4. Lettering can be guilded using silver or gold powder mixed with clear alcohol or use non-toxic gold or silver paint. Dry thoroughly before transferring to the cake.

Guilded Letters.

The runout letters are made in white and when dry painted gold or silver. Gold and silver comes in powder and liquid form. The powder has to be mixed with clear alcohol (gin, vodka, etc). Use the liquid in accordance with manufacturer's instructions.

The inscription shows a combination of pressure-piping on waxed paper. When dry stick on to cake surface and guild with a small paintbrush. The other lettering styles are piped with white icing directly onto the plaque and guilded when completely dry.

Direct piped Lettering

This plaque shows various inscriptions, all piped directly onto the surface with a No1 or 0 tube.

Blue Plaque

This simple plaque has a direct piped inscription and a decorative scroll piped with a No0 tube. The spray of flowers has piped royal icing leaves.

Painted Mimosa Plaque

Paint the mimosa leaves and stalks directly onto the plaque or cake, then pipe the 'Happy Birthday' inscription. The numbers are flooded in yellow and white. When dry, stick these on the plaque and finish off by piping 'today' freehand.

Pink Plaque

This plaque shows lettering piped in a circle with a No0 tube. When finished pipe tiny daisies in the centre. Alternatively, a posy of sugar or silk flowers could go into the centre, or make a runout design.

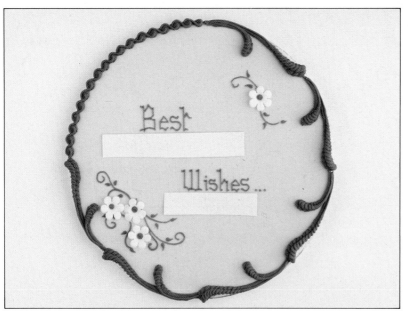

Round Plaque with Scroll Border

This plaque shows one technique for ensuring that lettering is straight. Cut thin strips of card or stiff paper and place on the cake or plaque surface. This gives a guideline to follow so you pipe in a straight line. Pipe shell and scroll edging with a No43 tube.

Dotted Lettering

This plaque shows different styles of lettering and numerals piped in dots. The name Cloe has a piped outline which is filled in with dots. The '18' and '21' and 'Best Wishes' are all piped directly onto the surface using a No. 1 tube.

The pressure-piped scroll lettering is piped in a No1 tube onto waxed paper. When dry the letters can be guilded in gold or silver or, as shown, with lustre colour mixed with clear spirit (gin, vodka, etc) and then painted over the surface. Leave to dry on the waxed paper, remove and stick on the surface with a little royal icing. A No5 tube was used for the shell edging to complete the plaque.

Monogram Plaque

This plaque shows three styles of monogram: runout, piped and painted. The R and J monogram is a runout. Trace the monogram onto tracing paper. Scribe onto the plaque or cake surface; outline with a No1 tube and flood in the monogram as shown in blue and yellow. Flood the back letter, leave to dry, then flood the second letter.

The piped monogram is started in the same way as the first, but it is not flooded for definition. Pipe using a contrasting colour to that used for the base of the cake.

The third monogram is painted. Draw monogram on tracing paper; scribe onto the surface. Paint with food colouring or with lustre colour.

Writing in a Circle

Writing in a circle looks good on a round cake. A posy or runout design could be placed in the centre of the circle. Pipe lettering before adding the centre decoration.

Place a round thin cake board on top of the cake. Make sure the board is large enough so that the centre decoration will fit. Decide on how much space the lettering will take up, then start piping. The tails of the Ps, Ys, and Gs are piped after the board is removed. Continue until the inscription is finished, remove the board and pipe any tails. Place the centre decoration in position.

Baby Plaque

This design would be suitable for a birth congratulations cake or christening cake. The main letters are direct-flooded runouts. Scribe the pattern on to the cake or plaque surface. Paint in the background using food colour mixed with clear spirit (gin, vodka, etc). Paint the stems of the foliage, the leaves and the cupids. Outline the B and W with No0 tube and flood in with pale pink royal icing. Leave to dry. Flood in the pillow and baby's head and paint in the blanket. The birds are pressure piped. Leave to dry, then position as shown. Paint the features on the baby's face. Use a small ejector to eject white blossom onto the plaque. Pipe the dots of pink icing into the centre of each blossom.

Pink Plaque

This plaque shows how to use plastic embossing script. Push the plastic piece into the paste covering of the cake or plaque within 15 minutes of coating, before a surface crust forms. Push into the paste in a straight movement – do not move about or you will get a distorted impression. Once pushed in, pull out straight to get a clean finish. When the impression is made you can leave it, or overpipe or outline the letters when the paste is dry.

Commercial Scripts.

This plaque shows a few of the many types of silver and gold plastic scripts and numerals available. These can be used on cakes or plaques. If you do not feel confident to write on a cake or are short of time these are an acceptable alternative.

Easter Plaque

This plaque would be suitable for an Easter cake, or the idea could be used for a child's name. Add pressure-piped animals or runout figures. The six letters are runouts. Leave to dry. Stick on to the cake surface with a little royal icing. Paint some grass along the base of the letters; pressure pipe the rabbits, as required, and then eject some mini-ejector blossom onto the grass.

Easter Cake

Detail of top of Easter Cake

Pressure-piped Rabbits

1. Pipe a bulb for the head.

2. Pipe the body. This is a large shell piped from the bottom upwards.

3. The ears and top part of the legs are piped on both using shell shapes.

4. Pipe in the feet, arms and the whiskers with a No0 tube. The body is textured with a fine paint-brush, either while piping or when the rabbit is finished. These rabbits can also be piped in miniature.

Easter Cake

Cover a 20cm (8in) square cake with pale lemon royal icing. Place on a 27.5cm (11in) square board.

Make a pattern for the large letter E by tracing onto tracing or greaseproof paper. Scribe the E on the cake surface. Outline with a dark yellow in a small bag fitted with a No1 tube, then flood with the same shade of runout icing.

Using a small cranked palette knife, smooth some green royal icing around the board. Place small mounds of sugarpaste on the sides of the cake, touching the board. Spread green royal icing over these, then, gently pat the surface with a piece of foam rubber. Dust blue petal dust around the side to make the sky.

Pressure-pipe some rabbits on the side. With a No1 tube in a small bag filled with green royal icing, pipe grass and flower stems, leaves around the edge. Eject some small ejector blossoms on the sides.

When the E is dry, dust some blue around it and paint a small butterfly. Pipe some stems with a No1 tube, using a small petal tube, pipe some daffodils directly onto the stems. Pipe in some leaves by cutting a V into the end of a bag. Spread some icing along the base of the E, then pipe the rest of the inscription with a No1 tube and pipe a pressure-piped rabbit.

Pipe a shell edging around the top edge to finish the cake.

The following scripts, figures, monograms and common words represent a good selection of lettering styles. Use in conjunction with the instructions in this chapter.

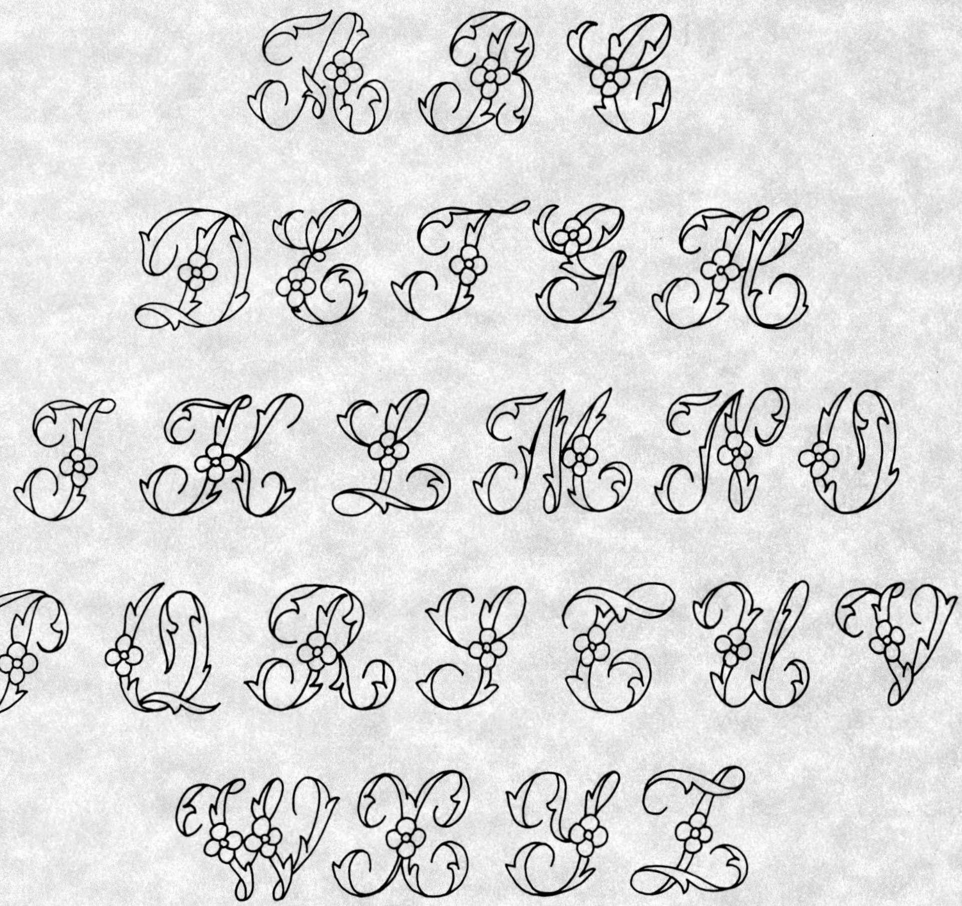

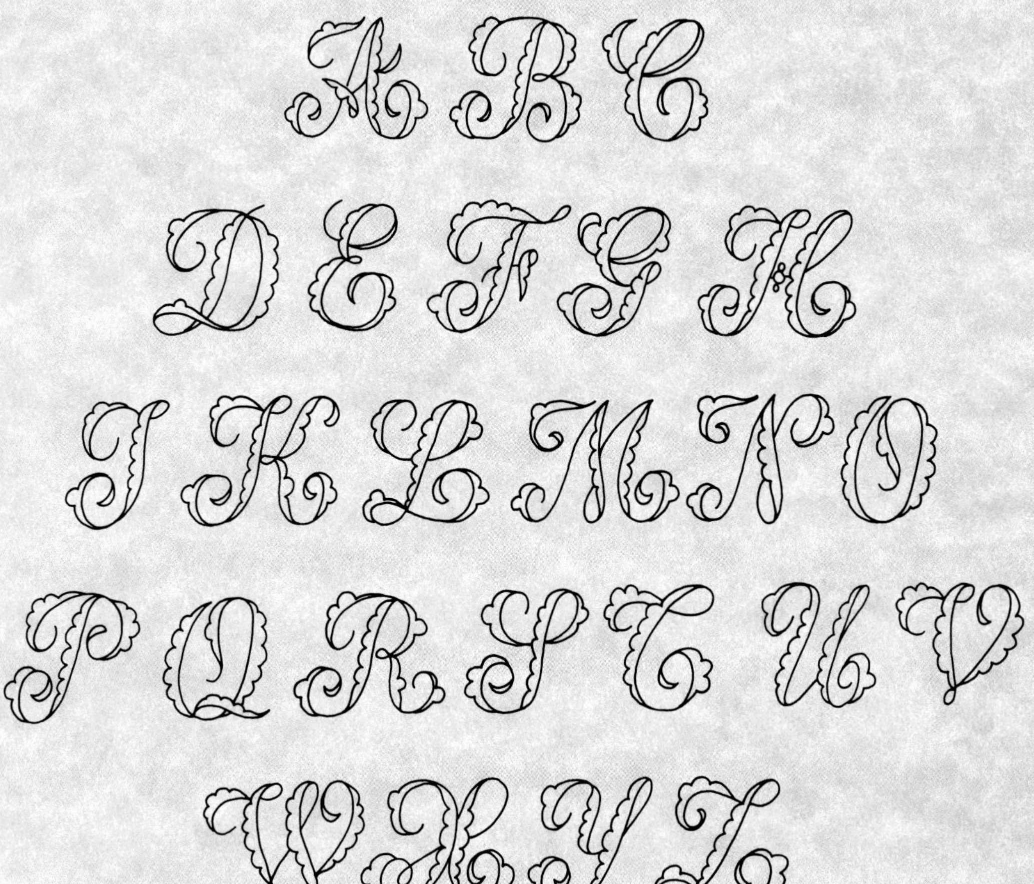

A B C
D E F G H
I K L M N O
P Q R S T U V
W X Y Z

A B C
D E F G H
I K L M N O
P Q R S T U V
W X Y Z

A B C D E F G
H I J K L M N
O P Q R S T U
V W X Y Z

a b c d e f g h i j k l m
n o p q r s t u v w x y z

A B C D E F G H I J K
L M N O P Q R S T U
V W X Y Z ~Mother~

ABCDEF
GHIJKL
MNOPQ
RSTUV
WXYZ

Mother   Kate

Anniversary

Father

ABCDEFGH
IJKLMNOP
QRSſ'ſTU
VWXYZ
1234567890

ABCDEFGHIJ
KLMNOPQR
STUVWXYZ
1234567890

ABCDEFGH
IJKLMNOP
QRSTUVW
XYZ

1234567890

1234567890

1234567890

1234567890

1234567890

1234567890

1234567 89

1234567890

1234567890

1234567890

Greetings

BEST WISHES

Best Wishes

Greetings

Greetings

GREETINGS

GREETINGS

Congratulations

Congratulations

Congratulations

Congratulations

Congratulations

Greetings

Greetings

Greetings

Greetings

Congratulations

G G G

Claire

On your 21st

S S

Easter

Congratulations on your Ruby Wedding

223

To My Valentine

21years

18

25

25

21

Congratulations
50
Golden years

50

Tulle

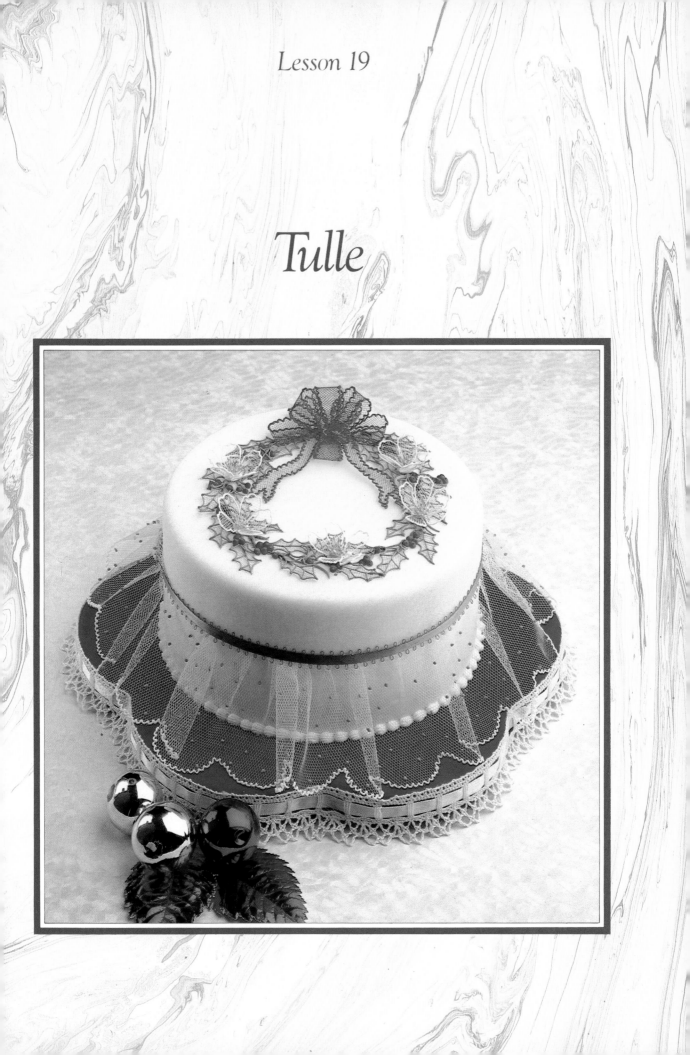

Tulle Work

Tulle piped with royal icing offers an interesting medium to the cake decorator, as the most delicate designs and flowers can be made.

Tulle comes in silk, cotton and synthetic fibres. Silk and cotton tulle are very expensive and difficult to obtain, so a synthetic tulle is a popular choice. For most work you will need the finest tulle available, which is bridal or veiling tulle available from a fabric or wedding shop in white, ivory and, occasionally, pastel colours.

You can dye the tulle with a fabric dye or food colouring. Soak the tulle in paste or liquid food colouring diluted with boiling water; (it is also possible to dye ribbons to match using this method). Once the tulle has been left to soak for 2-3 hours, lift out of solution and pat on a kitchen towel, then leave to dry. You will only get pale colours with food colour. If more vibrant colours are required, use a fabric dye and follow the manufacturer's instructions for use.

Tulle may also be coloured with petal dust, but again this is only suitable for very soft pastels.

Old bridal veils may sometimes be bought from second-hand shops for very little money and once washed, offer a cheaper alternative to buying new fabric.

Techniques
There are two basic styles for tulle work. The first uses flat cut-out pieces for such things as petals and leaves. The basic principle is to cut out the shape and, if drying flat, put it onto waxed paper or a lightly greased surface. The design is then piped freehand or by following a pattern placed under the waxed paper. Dry, remove and assemble or attach to cake surface. For curved pieces, attach the tulle on waxed paper to curve before piping, or place tulle over a greased surface.

If complicated designs are being piped and you need a pattern, pipe flat over the pattern and then place over a curved surface to dry. Work quickly, as the object must be wet when placed over the curve to prevent cracking. The second technique is for making tulle items such as christening robes, handkerchiefs, frills, etc. These are

sewn or folded, and then royal icing embroidery is piped on them. Work on a piece of foam if necessary. For objects like the robe, embroider the back, dry, then turn over and pipe the front last.

Frills
To make tulle frills, cut a strip of tulle two-and-a-half to three times the circumference of the cake. The depth will depend on the design. Once cut, fold up again and again until the piece is 2.5 to 5cm (1 to 2in). Cut one or two scallops. When the tulle is unfolded, the scallop edge is repeated along the length of the strip. Using a needle and thread, sew a running stitch along the other straight edge. When completed, tie thread around cake then stick the tulle down using a No1 tube with royal icing to match the shade of the covering. Make sure

the frills are even all the way around before sticking down. Place a ribbon over the join. Tulle frills can be left plain or embroidered.

Tulle Extension Work
As a simpler and much quicker alternative to piped extension work you can do tulle extension work. First of all decide on the shape; the work here is in a triangular pattern.

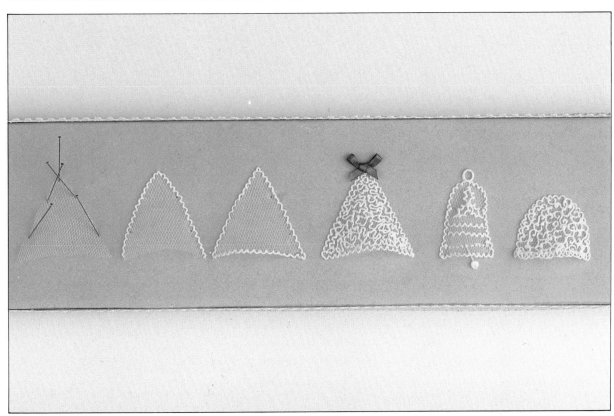

Bells and Oval Shapes

Cut out the tulle and pin onto the side of the cake. You will have to make a pattern so you know where to place each piece of tulle, either touching or slightly apart. Pipe a scalloped line along the edges, the icing should be right on the edge of the tulle so part of it touches the cake surface. Allow to dry. Pipe cornelli work all over the tulle and a scalloped line along the base. Finish off with a dropped line along the edge and place a tiny bow over the point.

Cut bell shapes, pipe in the same way as for triangular pieces. Pipe a clanger coming out of the bottom. The half oval also looks attractive on a shallow cake.

Narrow lilac frill

Cut a 2.5cm (1in) wide strip of tulle three times the circumference of the cake. Cut a scalloped edge, using a needle and thread put a running stitch along the straight edge of the strip. Gather, then stick around the side of the cake with royal icing. When dry, stick some pink and lilac ribbon above the frill, finishing off with a small bow in each colour. The embroidery on the tulle is piped with a No0 tube. Tiny dots are piped around the tulle and a scalloped line around the edge.

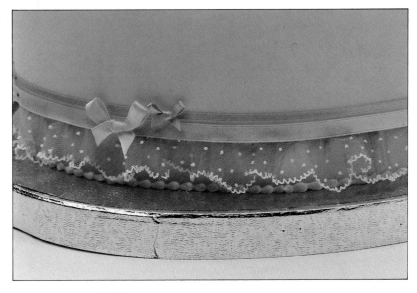

227

Wide Lilac Frills

This frill is approximately 5cm (2in) wide. Cut inverted scallops at regular intervals along the edge. Put a running stitch into the straight edge, gather and stick around the side of the cake. Embroider with tiny forget-me-nots and a scalloped line using a No0 tube. Finish off by sticking wide cotton lace above the tulle frill.

Butterfly

Cut out a pair of tulle butterfly wings using the template. Place the wings on a small piece of waxed paper. Pipe the design with a No0 tube and white icing. The design can be piped freehand or place a pattern under the template. Be sure the scalloped line on the edge has no gaps in it, or the wing may collapse. Dry the wings.

Pipe the body, using a No2 piping tube, directly on the cake surface or on a piece of waxed paper. Place the wings in the wet icing at once. Use a piece of foam or folded paper under each wing so that they dry at the angle you require.

Tiger Lily Petals

Cut out six orange petals for each lily using the template given. Lightly grease a former and stick the petals down over the former using a small dot of icing at each end. Using a No1 tube, pipe a scalloped line up both sides. Pipe three lines from the base up to approximately one-third of the length of the petal. Pipe in brown dots for the spots on the petals. Continue on all six petals.

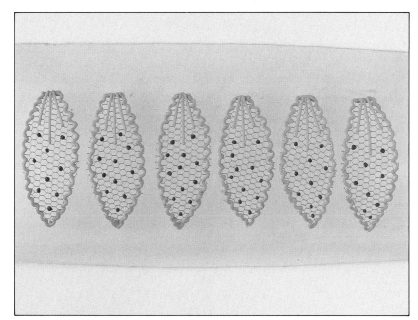

Tiger Lily Leaf

Cut out green tulle using the template. Place on a former and pipe a scalloped line along both edges. Pipe a straight line down the centre to support the leaf. Dry then reassemble around the tiger lilies. Assemble the tiger lily directly onto the cake surface or onto waxed paper. Pipe a bulb of orange royal icing and position the three base petals in a triangle. The next three petals are placed on top to fill in the three gaps left. Place six half-length stamens and one three-quarter-length stamen in the centre. Use large lily stamens brushed with brown royal icing over the ends.

Tulle Booties

These tulle booties have been piped in white on white tulle, but pastel tulle or icing could be used. The tiny bows could be in pink, blue or lemon.

A nice idea for using these is instead of a birth congratulations card. Put a pair of booties on a small plaque with a suitable inscription and give as a three-dimensional card, which could be placed in the nursery under a small glass dome. The booties look attractive on a christening cake.

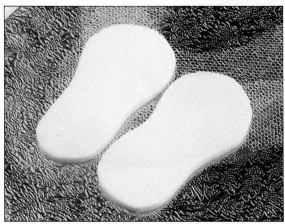

1. Roll out some sugarpaste or flower paste to approximately 3mm (¹⁄₁₀in) thick. Using the template given, cut out two soles with a scalpel or modelling knife. Turn one piece over so you have a pair of booties. Cut two tulle pieces for the tops.

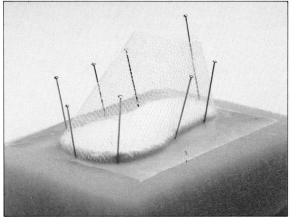

2. Place the soles on separate pieces of waxed paper and place on foam rubber. Using, a piping bag with No1 tube start at the back and stick the tulle edge to the sole. Use pins to help the tulle stick to the icing. Place the pins against the sole, but not into the paste. Thread a pin down the back of the tulle to hold together the heal end.

3. When the icing has dried, remove the pins by gently twisting each one. Use a No0 tube to cornelli all over the surface of the tulle.

4. Still keeping the bootie on the waxed paper, pipe a tiny shell around the base with the No0 tube. Finish with a miniature bow on each bootie.

Using white tulle, cut out the bodice using the template and cut a rectangle 40 x 12 cm (16 x 5″) for the skirt. Scallop one long edge of the rectangle and using a needle and thread, sew a line of running stitch close to the other edge. Pull the thread to gather up the tulle then sew the skirt to the bodice.

Attach blue, pink or lemon ribbon around the seam. A bow with long tails is sewn on the back and a tiny bow is sewn on the front.

Turn the robe over, place on foam rubber and start the embroidery. Use a No0 tube. Pipe scalloped lines around the bodice, with a row of bulbs to represent buttons. The main embroidery on the skirt is a rose and leaf pattern. When the flower embroidery is finished, pipe a scalloped line following the line of the hem. Tiny bows are piped on top of each one of the scallops. Leave to dry for about 30 minutes then turn over, place back on the foam, and embroider the front to match the back, except for the buttons. Leave to dry before placing on a cake.

Tulle Sprays

Tulle gives a soft effect when used in flower sprays. It softens harsh colours and flowers and fills in gaps in sprays or spaces around larger flat flowers like orchids and lilies. Choice of tulle is very important; use a very soft tulle like cotton or bridal tulle (veiling) so it folds into soft pleats. The coarser grade tulle will look very rigid and slightly harsh in sprays.

Making Tulle Sprays

1. Cut out a rectangle of tulle. The larger the rectangle the larger and longer the finished spray will be. An average size would be 7x12cm (3x5in).

2. Using your thumb and fingers, gather up the centre of the tulle along its length and hold in the the centre. Place a piece of 28-gauge wire over the centre. The wire should be approximately 15cm (6in) long.

3. Pull up both halves of the wire and twist firmly to secure. Trim off any excess tulle by pulling the sides back up and cutting with scissors. Pull out into a nice rounded shape.

Tulle and Pearl Sprays

These tulle sprays have pearls included in them and offer an alternative to plain tulle. Ribbons, feathers and silk flowers can also be wired in with tulle.

Handkerchief

Handkerchiefs look pretty in pastel colours with white piping. Tuck into a spray of flowers or place on top of a cake. Cut a square of tulle, fold into quarters and cut a large scalloped edge along both sides of the square. Open out and then fold in half diagonally, then fold the two sides under to get the shape shown. Pin together in several places. Embroider with a No0 tube. Pipe an oval cameo with an initial in the centre and daisy embroidery around the cameo. A line is then piped around the edge. Leave to dry before removing pins.

Heart

Cut out a tulle heart using the pattern given. Place on a piece of waxed paper and pipe a freehand embroidery design with a No1 tube. Similarly, a name could be piped or a runout attached. Use No5 tube to pipe a shell outline. When dry this heart can be used for the top of a cake. Make smaller hearts for the sides.

Posy Frill

This spray of fabric flowers in white, pink and green has been edged with a tulle posy frill.

Cut a strip of tulle 10cm (4in) wide and 40cm (16in) long. Fold in half and put a running stitch on the fold with a needle and thread. Fold in eight and cut a scalloped edge on the open side. Gather up the tulle and tie around the base of the flowers. Wrap a piece of fine wire around the posy to secure in place. With white royal icing and a No1 piping tube, pipe tiny dots all over the surface.

Briar Rose

Cut out five tulle petals for each rose from the template given. Place each petal on cupped foam as shown, pushing a pin into the centre of the tulle to cup it. Using a No1 tube, pipe a line around the tulle petals. Leave to dry. Once dry dust a little pink dusting powder at the base of each petal. Carefully pull out the pins using tweezers or fine-ended pliars.

Assemble the petals into a ring of icing piped on waxed paper or directly onto the cake surface. Support each petal with sponge pieces. Pipe some dots of bright yellow into the centre and place some yellow stamens into the wet icing. Leave to dry.

Rose Leaves

Cut out green tulle leaves.
Grease the surface of a former;
stick the broad end of the leaf
down. Using a No0 tube outline
the leaf shape. Never go over the
edge of the tulle. Pipe in the veins.
Dry, then attach to rose.

Bow Plaque

This plaque shows the steps for
making a tulle bow. Cut out the bow
pieces; two tails and one centre piece.
All the work is piped with a No0 tube.
Stick pieces into a bulb of royal icing,
folding one of each of the ends into
the centre. Pipe a scalloped line and
dots on the side pieces. Fold over the
two outer points and stick these into
the centre. Continue the piping onto
the top of the bow. Place the first tail
in position, piping a line around the
edge and dots to match the bow.
Place the second tail in position and
then fold the central piece into the
centre to finish off the tulle bow.

Loop bow

Cut out a loop of red tulle using the template. For the Christmas Cake featured you will need nine loops. Place a dot of icing onto waxed paper. Place one end of the tulle on the dot of icing. Pipe a scalloped line along both sides of the stuck-down end. Fold over the other side of tulle and stick on top of the first dot of icing. Continue piping the scalloped line on the top piece. Leave to dry.

Tails

Make one pair. Cut out tulle using the pattern. Pipe a scalloped line along the edge of piece. Reverse the other to make a pair and pipe as before.

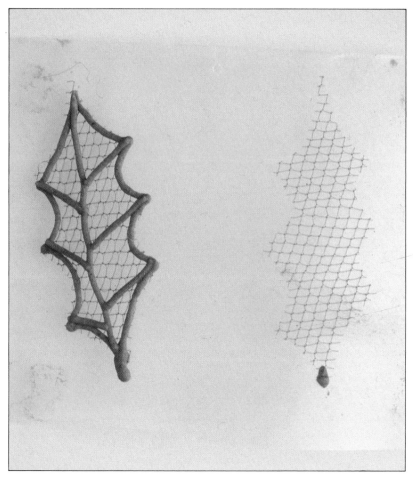

Holly Leaves

Cut out some green tulle following the holly leaf template. Pipe green outline and veins onto each leaf.

Ivy Leaves

Cut out the ivy leaves from green tulle using the template. Place on a curved surface. Pipe an outline and veins onto the leaves. Dry before use. These leaves look attractive with tulle flowers.

Christmas Rose

Cut out five petals for each rose from white tulle, using the template given. Place petals on waxed paper. Pipe an irregular straight line over the tulle to give a more natural effect to the petals. Dry the petals. When dry, pipe a circle of white royal icing, using a No1 tube, on another piece of waxed paper. Use a No0 tube to pipe bright yellow dots in the centre. While still soft position tiny yellow stamens with tweezers. When the flower is dry, dust a little moss green pètal dust into the centre.

Tulle
Christmas Cake

Prepare a petal-shaped board, covered in red velvet with white cotton lace around the edge. Bake a 15cm (6in) round cake, marzipan and cover in white sugarpaste. When covered place on a 15cm (6in) circle of waxed paper.

Place the cake with its circle of waxed paper onto the board. Paper stops the fruit cake from coming into direct contact with the velvet on the board.

Pipe a shell arond the base using a No42 piping tube. Use a 10cm (4in) board or cutter to mark a circle on the cake top for a guideline for the wreath.

Assemble the wreath. You will need approximately thirty tulle holly leaves, five christmas roses, nine bow loops and two tails. Use green royal icing to stick tulle pieces to the cake. Leave a 40mm (1½in) gap for the bow, which is assembled last. Stick five loops into a central bulb of icing, then place three more loops on top, and then one in the centre. To finish, position the tails into the bow to trail down the wreath. Pipe the holly berries in red.

Make a strip of tulle two-and-a-half times the circumference of the cake and approximately 6.5cm (2½in) wide and cut one side with a scalloped edge. Using a needle and thread, make a running stitch along the straight edge, and tie the tulle around the cake. Stick on using a No1 tube with white royal icing. You can use pins to hold tulle in position, but make sure that you remove them once icing is dry. Place a picot edge ribbon above the tulle, covering up the join. Embroider the tulle frill with tiny dots piped with a No1 tube and using green royal icing. To finish the frill pipe a scalloped line around the edge using a No0 tube and white icing. A suitable inscription could be written in the centre of the wreath, if liked.

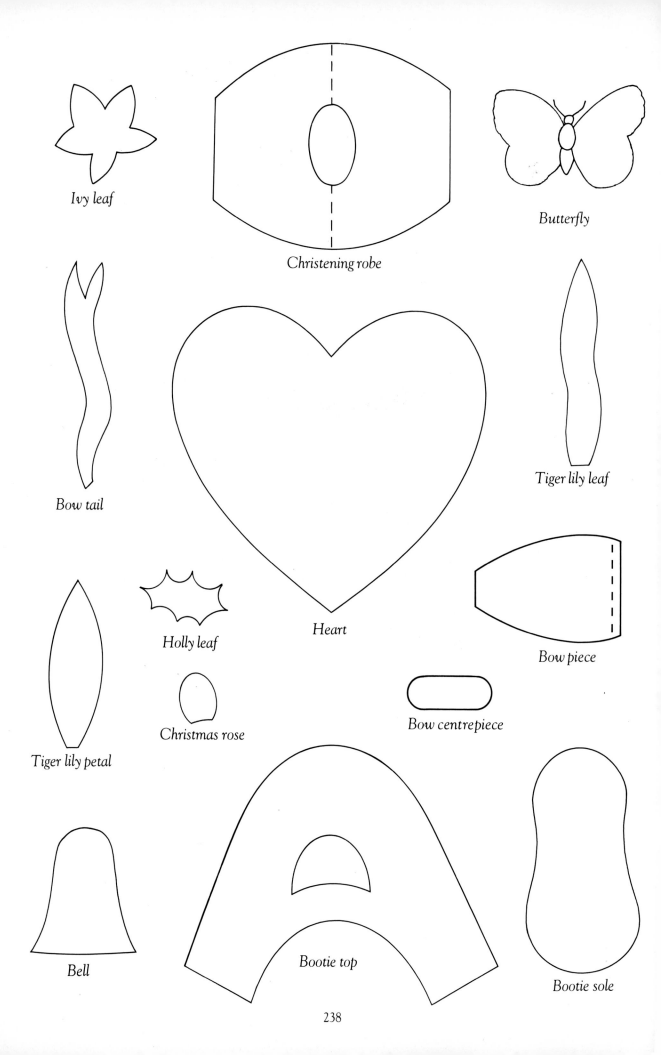

Ivy leaf

Christening robe

Butterfly

Bow tail

Tiger lily leaf

Holly leaf

Heart

Bow piece

Christmas rose

Bow centrepiece

Tiger lily petal

Bell

Bootie top

Bootie sole

238

Modelling

Modelling

Marzipan and sugarpaste can be used to model all sorts of shapes and figures to decorate cakes. Figure modelling is easy once the basic shapes have been learned, and even children can quickly create interesting and attractive models.

Use white marzipan for modelling, as it takes colour well. Home-made marzipan can be used, but commercial paste tends to be less sticky. Sugarpaste is easy to model and will roll without cracking, but because it is very soft, only simple, small figures can be made. If making more complicated figures, such as the clown, add gum tragacanth to make the paste stronger and more pliable. Use 5ml (1 teaspoon) for 250g (8oz) sugarpaste, knead thoroughly, then place in a plastic bag and rest for 2 hours before using.

When assembling figures, glue pieces together with a little egg white or with melted chocolate. Do not use cocktail sticks or wires on figures for children's cakes or party favours.

Equipment
Only a minimal amount of equipment is necessary for modelling, and often household tools can be adapted if special tools are unavailable. Most useful are a nonstick work surface and rolling pin; sharp kitchen knife; and a ball modelling tool. A crochet hook can be used instead of a ball tool.

Other modelling tools are available from cake decorating shops or from craft shops. Many tools used by potters are useful for marzipan modelling, as the techniques are quite similar.
All of the marzipan and sugarpaste figures are made using the some basic shapes. Practice each shape before trying out the figures. It is useful to measure out each piece so that you learn to recognise a 15g (½oz) ball, cone, etc, as this will help you to keep the pieces for each figure in proportion.

1. To make a ball, roll the marzipan between the lower part of the palms of your hands.

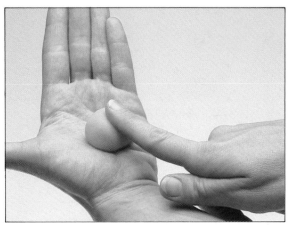

2. A butterbean shape is created when you place a ball in the palm of your hand and gently roll it with the index finger of your other hand.

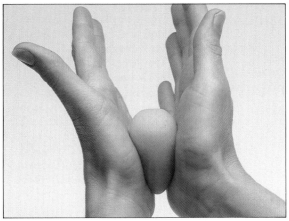

3. Form a cone by placing the ball at the base of your palms and move your hands backwards and forwards until the cone is smooth.

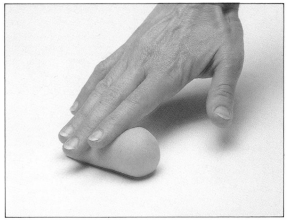

4. To make a elongated cone, place the cone on the work surface and roll the pointed end gently backwards and forwards.

5. To make a sausage shape, place the ball on the work surface and gently roll out, using two or three fingers.

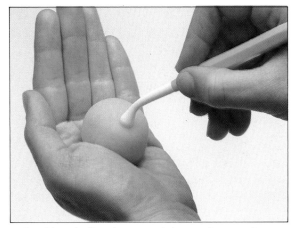

6. Use a ball tool or something similar to make indentations for eye sockets. Hold the ball of marzipan in one hand and gently press in the ball tool.

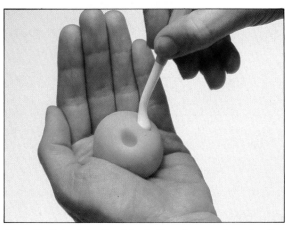

7. Pull the handle of the ball tool upwards and pull away quickly.

8. When making pieces for arms or legs, always make a ball first and then cut in half or in quarters to ensure even-sized pieces.

Sheep

Make a 4g (⅛oz) ball of black marzipan and cut in half. Make 15g (½oz) cone of white marzipan, with a slightly flattened end. Take one of the black pieces, roll into a ball and cut into four. Roll each one into a ball for the legs. Take the second black piece, save a little for the ears, then roll the rest into a cone and flatten to make head shape. Cut mouth using a modelling knife and make nostrils using a cocktail stick. Stick the four legs in position and place the head on the body. Using a small ball tool, make the eye cavities. Mould two small triangular ears and position. Using the clay gun, or a fine sieve or garlic crusher, with white marzipan make the fur. Attach all over the body. Pipe in the eyes using a No1 tube with white icing and let dry, then paint in black pupils.

Cat

This sweet little cat could be made in many colour combinations.

Make a 15g (½oz) ball. Cut into two pieces, one slightly larger than the other. Roll both pieces into balls, place the larger on the bottom for the body and the smaller one on top for the head. Press an oval of white sugarpaste on the front. Mould two upper and two lower legs and position. Mark the pads on the paws. Mould two small ovals and press on face for the cheeks. Mark a hole and use a half-scoop tool to mark the mouth. The nose is a pale pink ball; position and mark nostrils using a cocktail stick. Mark two indentations for the eyes using a ball tool. Place two triangular pieces for the ears; indent. Place some pink in each ear. Attach a long thin sausage tail. Place some white stamen cotton into the cheeks for whiskers. Pipe eyes with a No1 tube and, when dry, paint black with food colouring mixed with a little confectioner's varnish for the two pupils.

Mouse

This delightful little mouse can be used on many types of cakes and could be made larger is wished.

Make an 8g (¼oz) brown marzipan cone shape with quite a tapered end, then bend the end over for the head. Make two indentations for the ears, mould and attach the ears. Make two indentations for the eyes. Attach a pink rose. Place three pieces of stamen cotton on each side for the whiskers. Cut a small ball in half and mould two arms. For the apron, roll out some white paste, cut out a small circle, cut off the top, then frill the edges using a cocktail stick. Stick on with egg white. Cut a small rectangle of paste, place above the frilled piece for the top of the apron. Roll two thin white sausages and place one around the neck and one around the body. Trim off excess. Make a bow out of a thin sausage of paste and stick on back. Position a small pocket and add a little pink marzipan handkerchief. Attach arms. Finish off by piping in the eyes. When dry paint in pupils. Make a tiny basket filled with miniature apples or flowers to go over one arm.

Goose

Make a 15g (½oz) ball. Mark into quarters and cut out a quarter section. Make the three-quarter piece into a cone shape. Elongate the thin end into the neck. Make a bulb for the head. Squash the rounded end and cut into four. Curl over to give the effect of tail feathers. Make two eye identations using a small ball tool and with the same tool make an indentation for the beak. Taking the remaining quarter section, cut in half, and put one piece back in the pack. The remaining piece is cut into two. Roll each piece into a ball and squash for the wings. Mark the feathers and attach wings to the body. Mould a yellow piece for the beak and attach. Make two orange pieces for the feet; mark the webbing with a cocktail stick. Attach.

Chicken

Make a 15g (½ oz) orange-brown marzipan cone. Elongate the neck. Make a bulb for the head. Flatten the other end for the tail. Cut the tail feathers with small scissors, then roll around the paintbrush to curl. Use a half-scoop modelling tool to mark the feathers all over, except on the head. Make a small ball of orange-brown paste and cut in half for wings. Thin each piece between your fingers and attach to the body. Use the scoop tool to mark the feathers and help join the wings to the body. Make a small piece of red marzipan and mould the cockscomb and gisard and place into position. Place two small pieces on either side of the face and flatten. Make the beak from yellow paste. Make indentations for eyes. Pipe the eyes using white icing. When dry paint in black pupils. The feet are cut from a thin sausage and attached. Mould two or three eggs. Dust yellow on the breast of the chicken.

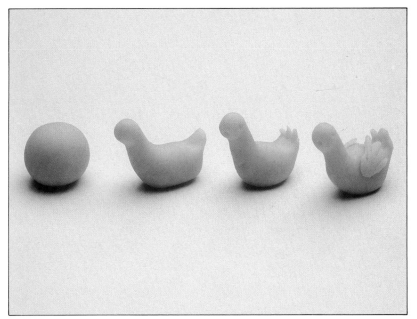

Pig

Make a 22g (¾oz) pink cone. Drag the narrow end across the work surface to flatten for the snout, turn and pull the nose up. Cut the mouth with a small sharp knife and mark the two nostrils using a ball tool. Make a ball of paste and cut into four. Mould each one into a ball and position for the legs. Make indentations for the eyes and ears in the front and indent the back for the tail. Mould and position. Mould the tail and place into the cavity. Pipe in the whites of eyes using a No1 tube, and paint the brown pupils when dry.

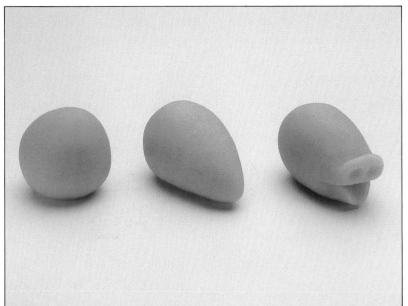

Goat and Cow

These are made in the same way, although the faces are a little different. Pull up one end for the neck and make a bulb for the head. Pull them up and out. The back is pinched slightly to give a ridge. Mould the tail by pulling a piece from the back end of the sausage. Make two indentations each side for the legs to sit in. Squash in thin sausages of white marzipan for markings. Cut mouth, make two ears and two eye sockets. Make some indentations down front. Make small gruff to go under the goat's chin. Place a piece of white above the tail. Make four sausages for legs. The back ones are only two-thirds full length as they sit under the body. Pipe the whites of the eyes with a No1 tube; paint black pupils in when dry.

247

Farmer

Trousers: Make a 15g (½oz) blue sausage. Cut in half two-thirds of the way up to represent the legs. Mould to make rounded. Make a small cavity in each of the ends for the shoes to sit in.

Shoes: Make a small brown ball. Cut in half and mould into shoe shapes. Make two little pegs to hold shoes to trousers. Stick together and lay down on foam to dry.

Head: Make a flesh-coloured ball with a slight piece moulded down for the neck. Mould a nose and place into indentations. Use a half-scoop tool to mark the mouth. The eye cavities are made using a small ball tool.

Shirt: Make a 15g (½oz) cone shape.

Cap and crook: Mould a long thin sausage for the crook. The cap is a flattened ball with a small piece on the front for the peak. Mark the lines on top with a small knife.

Arms and shirt top: Cut a ball in half and mould into a sausage. Using a ball tool, make an indentation into each end of the sausage and place cone-shaped arm in each.

Assembling: Stick trousers and top together. Make waistcoat out of green marzipan by rolling and then cutting out the shape. A brown belt is put around his waist. Make a cavity for his neck to sit in and place his head in position. Paint hair using food colouring and then put on cap. Tie a red scarf around neck. Dust cheeks pink and paint in lips. Pipe in white of eyes with a No1 tube, then paint in his pupils using a fine paintbrush. Mould 2 tiny ears and place one either side of his head.

Farmyard Birthday Cake

Marzipan and royal ice a 20cm (8in) square cake. The first two coats are white. Coat the sides only with two further coats in blue icing. Dry thoroughly.

Scribe a line along the four sides using a scriber and ruler. Place the ruler against the side with one edge resting on the board and scribe a line along the top edge. Using green food colour diluted with clear spirit (gin, vodka), paint grass around the edge.

Pipe four fence pieces onto waxed paper following the template. Use brown icing without glycerine and No2 piping tube. Leave to dry. Using a small cranked palette knife, spread green icing on the board and over the edge then pat with a piece of foam to give a stippled effect. Leave to dry. Tilt each side in turn and position the fence pieces. Dry. Using white icing and a No1 tube, pipe the clouds, then use foam or a paint brush to fluff them up. Pipe grass up fence using a No0 tube. Add small ejector blossoms for the flowers. Pipe birds in the sky.

Top assembly
Make four fence pieces following the template. Spread some green icing on to the top of the cake leaving a small white area for the inscription. Remove the four dry fence panels, and stick the first along the back of the cake with a line of green icing. The second piece goes along the right-hand side of the cake, the third along the front and the fourth is attached at the join of the first, but left open, as shown. Pipe some brown icing with a No1 tube around tops to look like rope. Place the sheep in the pen and the farmer in position. Pipe the inscription in the white area and pipe a border along top edges. If liked, position other marzipan animals around the board.

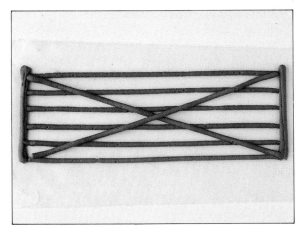

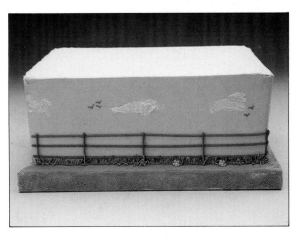

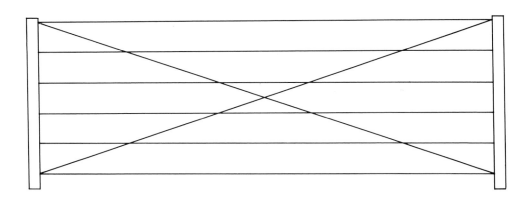

Sugarpaste and Marzipan Roses

The roses can be made in any size from sugarpaste or marzipan. The principle is the same. If you are using sugarpaste, knead in a little white fat (shortening). You can leave the rose at any of the first three stages, making it into a bud, medium or a larger rose. The size of the cone and ball of paste for the petals will determine the size of the finished rose.

1. Mould a cone of paste.

2. Take a piece of paste, roll into a ball and then place between a folded piece of polythene.

3. Thin out the petal edges. Remove from polythene and wrap around the cone, enclosing the cone completely. Waist in cone to establish shape.